Strange Indiana Monsters

Michael Newton

Schiffer Publishing Ltd
4880 Lower Valley Road, Atglen, PA 19310 USA

Published by Schiffer Publishing Ltd.
4880 Lower Valley Road
Atglen, PA 19310
Phone: (610) 593-1777; Fax: (610) 593-2002
E-mail: Info@schifferbooks.com

For the largest selection of fine reference books on this and related subjects,
please visit our web site at **www.schifferbooks.com**
We are always looking for people to write books on new and related subjects.
If you have an idea for a book please contact us at the above address.

This book may be purchased from the publisher.
Include $3.95 for shipping.
Please try your bookstore first.
You may write for a free catalog.

In Europe, Schiffer books are distributed by
Bushwood Books
6 Marksbury Ave.
Kew Gardens
Surrey TW9 4JF England
Phone: 44 (0) 20 8392-8585; Fax: 44 (0) 20 8392-9876
E-mail: info@bushwoodbooks.co.uk
Website: www.bushwoodbooks.co.uk
Free postage in the U.K., Europe; air mail at cost.

Designed by John P. Cheek
Cover design by Bruce Waters
Type set in Bernhard Modern BT/Souvenir Lt BT

ISBN: 0-7643-2608-2
Printed in China

Dedication

For Zöe

Contents

Map of Indiana 6

Acknowledgements 7

Introduction: What is Cryptozoology? 8

Chapter 1. Hypothetical Inhabitants 12

Chapter 2. Rampant Reptiles 26

Chapter 3. Oscar—The Beast of 'Busco 33

Chapter 4. Phantom Cougars 41

Chapter 5. Alien Big Cats.................................... 48

Chapter 6. Lake Monsters 59

Chapter 7. Tentacles 70

Chapter 8. Kangaroos, Devil Monkeys, and NAPEs 75

Chapter 9. Bigfoot 80

Chapter 10. Stranger Yet...................................... 99

Endnotes 109

Sources...

INDIANA - Counties

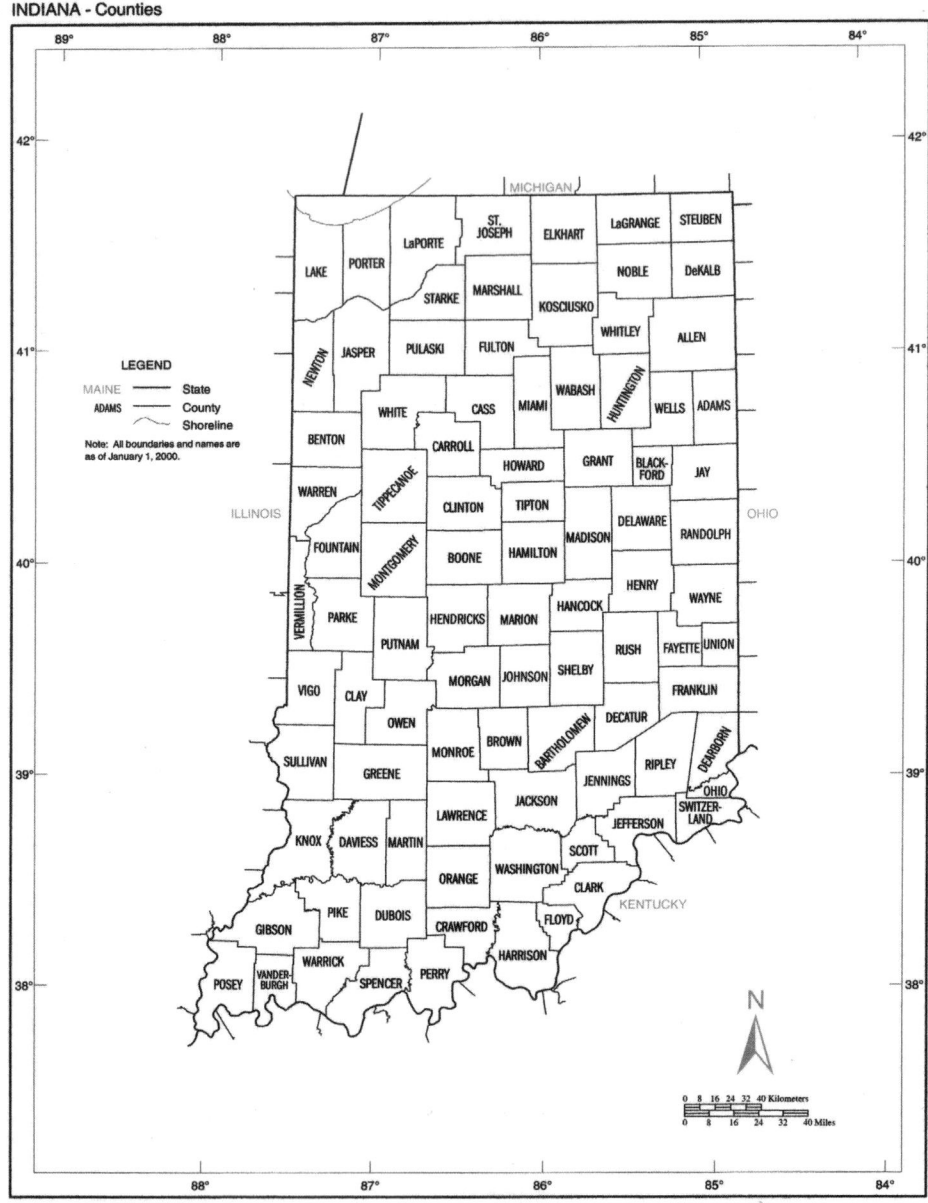

Acknowledgements

I owe a debt of gratitude to many people, without whom the work in hand might not exist. They include David Frasier, longtime friend and researcher *par excellence,* for his generous assistance on this project, as with countless others; Tom Alberts, with the *Shelbyville News;* Lisa Allen, at the *Anderson Herald Bulletin;* Marvin Allen, Starke County historian; author Chad Arment; Mike Bardsley, Indiana Bigfoot Awareness Group; Ron Hamilton, journalist and historian of Shelby County, Indiana; Carol Utter Johnson, of Rochester; Jeff Kenney, Culver-Union Township Public Library; Jesse Lewis, Indiana State Library; John Lutz, founder and head of the Eastern Puma Research Network; Paul McLean, Falls of the Ohio State Park; Beth Oljace, Anderson Public Library; Sandy Parker, Rochester & Lake Manitou Chamber of Commerce; John Plowman, with the *Pulaski Journal;* Katie Smith, with Indiana's Department of Natural Resources; Shirley Willard, Fulton County historian; Carol Young, of Mission, Texas; Sue Zellers, Knox County Historical Society; Rob Ziessler, Plymouth Public Library; and my wife Heather, for her editorial advice, her photographs, and her boundless patience. Thanks also to my editor, Dinah Roseberry, for her enthusiasm and support.

INTRODUCTION
What is Cryptozoology?

In 1957, Belgian zoologist Bernard Heuvelmans coined the term, *cryptozoology*, defined as the study of "hidden" animals—i.e., creatures unrecognized by modern science. When the International Society of Cryptozoology was organized in 1982, with Heuvelmans as president, the founders proclaimed that cryptozoology also concerns "the possible existence of *known* animals in areas where they are not supposed to occur (either now or in the past) as well as the unknown persistence of presumed extinct animals to the present time or to the recent past. What makes an animal of interest to cryptozoology...is that it is *unexpected*."[1]

Hidden or unexpected animals—commonly called *cryptids*—are not "unknown;" rather, their existence, in most cases, is officially unverified. In 1985, the late J. Richard Greenwell proposed a classification system for cryptids, including the following groups:[2]

(1) Members of a known, living species whose form, size, color or pattern is extraordinary for its species (e.g., reports of giant anacondas in Brazil).

(2) Extant and well-known species unrecognized as living in a particular area (e.g., kangaroos in North America).

(3) Presumably extinct species, not fossil forms, known only from limited organic evidence (skin, feathers, etc.), but without a complete type specimen.

(4) Known species presumed extinct within historical times, which may have survived to the present day (e.g., Australian thylacines).

Giant anacondas are reported from Brazil's Amazon basin. *Courtesy of William Rebsamen.*

Although officially extinct, thylacines are still reported from Australia. *Courtesy of William Rebsamen.*

(5) Representatives of fossil forms presumed extinct during geologic times, which may have survived into historical times or to the present day (e.g., the coelacanth).

The "extinct" coelacanth was found alive and well in 1938. *Courtesy William Rebsamen.*

(6) New species known from anecdotal evidence, for which no known organic evidence exists.

(7) New species previously unreported or known to aboriginal people, which may be accidentally discovered (e.g., the megamouth shark).

Strange Indiana Monsters reviews, for the first time in book form, the history and broad scope of cryptozoology in Indiana. It does not, as Dr. Heuvelmans declared in 1982, present "an arcane or occult zoology."[3] Nothing here pertains to any aspect of the supernatural. That said, however, there is no shortage of mysteries to be explored.

The work in hand consists of ten chapters, topically arranged.

Chapter 1 briefly examines Indiana's recognized wildlife plus various "hypothetical" species still unacknowledged by state authorities.

Chapter 2 presents evidence of exotic reptiles seen—and sometimes caught—within the Hoosier State.

Chapter 3 visits the Beast of 'Busco, to discover whether giant turtles dwell in Indiana's lakes.

Chapter 4 reviews compelling evidence for the local survival of cougars, presumed extinct in Indiana for 150 years.

Chapter 5 describes Indiana sightings of Alien Big Cats (ABCs), including "African" lions and so-called "black panthers."

Chapter 6 proceeds with a survey of reported Hoosier lake monsters.

Chapter 7 reports the appearance of cephalopods in Indiana, far from their normal marine habitats.

Chapter 8 evaluates reports of kangaroos at large and offers some startling explanations for those sightings.

Chapter 9 collects 170 years of Bigfoot/Sasquatch sightings logged throughout Indiana. Finally,

Chapter 10 dissects reports of various fantastic beasts including dragons, flying headless monsters, lizard men and werewolves that have frightened Indiana residents for well over a century.

Chapter 1
HYPOTHETICAL INHABITANTS

According to the Indiana Academy of Sciences and the state's Department of Natural Resources (DNR), Indiana harbors 807 recognized species of wild vertebrates, including 208 fish, 38 amphibians, 54 reptiles, 401 birds and 68 mammals. Of those 807 species, 101—or 12.5 percent—are presently threatened or endangered by human conduct. Thirty-two other species previously found in Indiana have been extirpated by humans since the early nineteenth century, including ten fish, one snake, eight birds, and thirteen mammals. Of those thirty-two, three—the beaver (*Castor canadensis*), river otter (*Lutra canadensis*), and white-tailed deer (*Odocoileus virginianus*)—were subsequently reintroduced. White-tails now rank as abundant statewide, while beavers are common, and otters remain rare.[1]

Official documents describe eleven other vertebrate species as "hypothetical," meaning that witnesses have logged encounters during recent times, but their reports are unconfirmed. That list includes six amphibians, three reptiles, and two mammals.[2] While none of them qualify as "monsters," discovery of verified specimens for any or all of the uncertain species would rank as a feather in the cap of some amateur cryptozoologist.

"Hypothetical" Species

Indiana's hypothetical amphibians include the bird-voiced treefrog (*Hyla avivoca*), the green treefrog (*H. cinerea*), the mountain chorus frog (*Pseudacris brachyphona*), the eastern narrowmouth toad (*Gastrophryne carolinensis*), the mud salamander (*Pseudotriton montanus*), and the spring salamander (*Gyrinophilus porphyriticus*).[3]

Brief descriptions follow:

Hyla avivoca is a small swamp-dweller, its largest known specimen measuring just over two inches long. Its mottled skin, in shades of green, includes light patches underneath both eyes, with paler green or yellowish-white beneath its rear legs. It is easily mistaken for the somewhat larger gray treefrog (*H. versicolor*), found throughout Indiana, but its northernmost range—including southern Illinois and northwestern Kentucky—does not officially include the Hoosier State. *H. avioca*'s call is a distinctive, rapid "wit-wit-wit," repeated twenty times or more in a high-pitched, chirping chorus.[4]

Hyla cinerea is a slightly larger treefrog, with a maximum recorded length of 2.5 inches. A pale lateral stripe separates its green dorsal side and pale underbelly. Some sources grant *H. cinerea* a small population in far-southern Indiana, but state authorities refuse to confirm its existence.[5]

The Ohio River separates *Pseudacris brachyphona*'s normal range in Kentucky from southern Indiana, but sporadic Hoosier sightings suggest that it may occasionally cross that barrier. Coloration varies widely from the reddish-brown norm, with black stripes through the eyes suggesting a burglar's mask. Dark spots also decorate the yellow groin of this small frog, whose maximum recorded length is 1.9 inches.[6]

Gastrophryne carolinensis inhabits most of the southeastern United States, encroaching on Indiana from northern Kentucky. Its maximum official length of 1.5 inches accommodates a round body, generally brown or gray in color, with the small pointed head seeming tiny by comparison.[7]

Gyrinophilus porphyriticus invades Indiana, if at all, from an isolated population in western Ohio, roughly adjacent to Dearborn and Ohio Counties. The largest known specimen measured 9.1 inches, while average adults range from 4.75 to 7.5 inches. Uniform reddish-brown coloration is punctuated by small, darker spots along both sides.[8]

Our last hypothetical amphibian, *Pseudotriton montanus,* inhabits the southern bank of the Ohio River, in Kentucky and Ohio, but allegedly mimics *Pseudacris brachyphona* by fording the stream on occasion.

While smaller than *Gyrinophilus porphyriticus,* boasting a record length of 8.1 inches and an average maximum of 6.5 inches, this is a more colorful salamander, brighter reddish-brown, with dark spots covering its back and sides.[9]

Indiana's three hypothetical reptiles include the coal skink (*Eumeces anthracinus*), Graham's water snake (*Regina grahamii*), and the lined snake (*Tropidoclonian lineatum*).[10] As with the six amphibians described above, none officially inhabit Indiana, but one is found in territory bordering the Hoosier State.

Coal skinks are average-sized lizards, measuring five to seven inches long as adults. Despite their name, they are not black, but rather boast light-colored stripes on each side, separated by a wider dark stripe, running laterally from the eye to the midpoint of the tail. They inhabit wooded hillsides, rocky bluffs and creek valleys—but unlike the reptiles considered below, their normal ranges in Kentucky and Ohio do not abut Indiana's border.[11]

Regina grahamii, also known as Graham's crayfish snake, averages 20-30 inches long, with a record length of 36.5 inches. Its range in Illinois borders Lake Michigan, around Chicago, and may thus—at least in theory—encroach on far-northwestern Indiana. Dining almost exclusively on crayfish, *R. grahamii* lives close to water. Its dark dorsal surface may be marked by lighter stripes, while the underside is a more-or-less uniform yellow.[12]

The more colorful lined snake closely resembles its relatives, the garter and ribbon snakes (genus *Thamnophis*). It measures 8.75 to 15 inches in adulthood, with a record length of 21.5 inches. Dorsal stripes vary in color from pale gray or white to yellow and orange, while a double row of bold, black half-moon patterns mark the snake's belly. Commonly found in the central United States from Texas to the Dakotas, its scattered habitats in Illinois do not touch Indiana's border.[13]

Two species of mammals sometimes reported from Indiana, but officially nonexistent there, are the eastern harvest mouse (*Reithro-*

dontomys humulis) and Leib's bat (*Myotis leibi*).[14] Both occupy similar ranges adjacent to the Hoosier State, but are denied official recognition by the DNR.

Reithrodontomys humulis is an ordinary-looking mouse, ranging from 4.25 inches to 5 inches long (tail included), weighing 10-15 grams. It thrives in meadows, marshlands, and weedy irrigation ditches throughout eastern Kentucky and southern Ohio, but theoretically never finds its way across the Ohio River into Indiana, despite unconfirmed eyewitness reports.[15]

Leib's bat, also known as the small-footed myotis, ranks among North America's smallest bat species. It dwells in the coniferous and deciduous forests of Kentucky and Ohio, but like the eastern harvest mouse and other species, does not officially occur in Indiana. Despite its small size—weighing 3 to 7 grams, with an average wingspan of 2.7 to 3.25 inches—Leib's bat may live for 12 years (compared to 18 months or less for other small rodents).[16]

Dead and Gone?

Regrettable confusion surrounds the number and identity of Indiana's extirpated species. While state authorities list thirty species wiped out by humans—ten fish, one snake, eight birds, and eleven mammals—Hoosier outdoor writer Harold Allison claims five more extirpated birds disputed by the DNR (including one ranked as common on state wildlife lists).[17] We shall consider each in turn and leave the field research to naturalists with a taste for outdoor exploration.

Indiana's only extirpated reptile is the western mud snake (*Farancia abacura*), officially wiped out in 1894. It still survives in southern Illinois and far-western Kentucky, while one field guide locates a viable population in southwestern Indiana. Another snake, the venomous cottonmouth (*Agkistrodon piscivorus*), was once believed extinct but now rates listing as a threatened species in southern Indiana. America's largest turtle, the alligator snapper (*Macroclemys temminicki*), was likewise once believed to be extinct in Indiana, but lingers with an "endangered" rating in isolated pockets unrecognized by most field guides.[18]

No doubt apparently surrounds three of Indiana's eight officially extirpated birds: Bachman's warbler (*Vermivora bachmanii*), the Eskimo curlew (*Numenius borealis*), and the whooping crane (*Grus americana*) are now regarded by all experts as extinct. Two others ranked as nonexistent in the Hoosier State—the gray partridge (*Perdix perdix*) and the greater prairie chicken (*Tympanuchus cupido*)—survive today in other states, including a recognized population of *T. cupido* in eastern Illinois, abutting Indiana's Gibson and Posey Counties.[19]

Two other species formerly seen in Indiana, the Carolina parakeet (*Conuropsis carolinensis*) and the ivory-billed woodpecker (*Campephilus principalis*), were seemingly extirpated in the twentieth century. A Florida hunter killed the last confirmed pair of Carolina parakeets in April 1904, while the last captive specimen died at Cincinnati's zoo on February 1918. The ivory-bill proved more durable, its last officially confirmed sighting reported from Louisiana in 1943. Unverified parakeet sightings continued in Dixie through 1937, while living ivory-bills were reported from the southern United States and Cuba through 1999. In April 2005, searchers in Arkansas astounded the scientific world with a four-second videotape of a living ivory-billed woodpecker. Despite that evidence, some skeptics insist that recent sightings actually involve the similar, but smaller, pileated woodpecker (*Dryocopus pileatus*), which lacks the ivory-bill's distinctive white beak.[20]

Harold Allison confused the avian question in August 2001, with a newspaper article naming five more bird species as extinct in Indiana. His list included the common loon (*Gavia immer*), the common raven (*Corvus corax*), the double-crested cormorant (*Phalacrocorax auritus*), the swallow-tailed kite (*Elanoides forficatus*), and Wilson's phalarope (*Phalaropus tricolor*). National Geographic's *Field Guide to the Birds of North America* agrees with Allison on four counts, excluding a small cormorant population located in southwestern Indiana, but state authorities dispute the status of all five species. The DNR ranks loons as "common" in the Hoosier State, and double-crested cormorants as "occasional," while ravens, kites and Wilson's phalarope are "rare."[21]

The Carolina parakeet is presumed to be extinct. *Courtesy U. S. Fish and Wildlife Dept.*

The "extinct" ivory-billed woodpecker was rediscovered in 2005. *Courtesy U. S. Fish and Wildlife Dept.*

Debate continues in regard to five of Indiana's eleven extirpated mammals, including the black bear (*Ursus americanus*), the cougar (*Puma concolor*), the eastern spotted skunk (*Spiligale putorius*), the porcupine (*Erethizon dorsatum*), and the gray wolf (*Canis lupus*).[22] Surviving cougars are discussed in Chapter 3, but the remaining species rate examination here.

While Indiana hunters officially annihilated black bears in 1850, gray wolves in 1908, porcupines in 1918, and spotted skunks around 1920, sightings of all four species continue to the present day. In fact, the Smithsonian Institution acknowledges a small porcupine population in southwestern Indiana, but finds none of the others present. Black bears allegedly come no closer to Indiana than northern Michigan and southwestern Kentucky, spotted skunks stray no nearer than eastern Kentucky, and gray (or timber) wolves lurk only along the Canadian border, in far-northern Michigan.[23]

Nonetheless, Harold Allison reported in August 2001 that his private files contained "about a dozen" Indiana black bear sightings, two spotted skunk reports, two porcupine sightings from northeastern Indiana's Pigeon River region, and twelve sightings of "gray wolf like creatures" statewide. In May 2004, Allison reported three new bear reports, for a total of eight counties with sightings on file. The presence of at least one gray wolf was confirmed in early August 2003, when an unknown gunman illegally killed it near Winchester, but federal authorities traced the tagged specimen to a pack in Wisconsin's Black River State Forest. Suggested explanations for Indiana's other wolf sightings include misidentification of feral dogs or various hybrid species.[24]

Black bears are officially extinct in Indiana, yet sightings continue. *Courtesy U. S. Fish and Wildlife Dept.*

Wolf sightings persist, although none officially survive in the Hoosier State. *Courtesy U. S. Fish and Wildlife Dept.*

Porcupines, also "extinct" in Indiana, still surface on occasion. *Courtesy U. S. Fish and Wildlife Dept.*

Alien Invaders

Aside from extirpated species that refuse to fade away, Indiana also hosts a plethora of "exotics"—non-native (and frequently unwelcome) species imported from other states or countries. By March 2005, an estimated 4,500 exotic species were recognized in the United States, from coast to coast. Most of those alien invaders were plants or insects, but the total included fifty-three reptiles and amphibians, ninety-seven birds, and twenty mammals. (No tally was offered for exotic fish.) Various native species also rank as exotic when found in states outside their normal range. Officially, the Hoosier State now harbors thirty-four exotic species, including twenty-three fish, nine birds, and two mammals.[25] As we shall see, however, that census is only the tip of the iceberg.

Exotic fish species ranked "abundant" by the DNR include the alewife (*Alosa pseudoharengus*), the carp (*Cyprinus carpio*), and the round goby (*Neogobius melanostomus*). Those rated "common" include the brown trout (*Salmo trutta*), Chinook salmon (*Oncorhynchus tshawytscha*), Coho salomon (*O. kisutch*), goldfish (*Carassius auratus*), rainbow smelt (*Osmerus mordus*), rainbow trout (*Oncorhynchus mykiss*), and threadfin shad (*Dorosoma petenense*). "Occasional" species include the Atlantic salmon (*Salmo salar*), bighead carp (*Hypophthalmichthys nobilis*), grass carp (*Ctenopharyngodon idella*), red shiner (*Cyprinella lutrensis*), sea lamprey (*Petromyzon marinus*), striped bass (*Morone axatilis*), threespine stickleback (*Gasterosteus aculeatus*), and white catfish (*Ameiurus catus*). Rare exotic fish in Hoosier lakes and streams include the rudd (*Scardinus erythophthalmus*), inland silverside (*Menidia beryllina*), striped mullet (*Mugil cephalus*), white perch (*Morone americana*), and silver carp (*Hypophthalmichthys molitrix*).[26]

These well-established aliens are not Indiana's only aquatic invaders, however. On August 27, 2000, fisherman Dave Smiejek pulled an eleven-inch piranha (*Serrasalmus* sp.) from Flint Lake, near Valparaiso, while companion Patrick Gibbs reported seeing a school of eight similar fish the same day. DNR records include seven piranha retrieved from a city park pond in Boone County (July 2002), two ten-inch specimens pulled from the White River, in Delaware County (August 2002), and a lone piranha hooked at Cedar Lake (August 2002). Stories of multiple captures from ponds in Delaware County remain unconfirmed. Reporter Howard Allison claims knowledge of "at least five sites in southern Indiana" where anglers have caught live piranhas, plus unspecified additional reports of free-swimming schools.[27] Needless to say, the presence of voracious South American "cannibal fish" in Hoosier waters gives cause for concern.

Another possible piranha catch was logged from Griffy Lake, near Bloomington, in July 2001. Fisherman Jack Goe pronounced himself "99-percent sure" that his 14-inch, 2.5-pound trophy was a genuine piranha, but Indiana University professor of biology Bill Rowland opined that it might be a harmless look-alike cousin, the pacu (*Colossoma macropomum*). DNR agents accepted that judgment, while other definite pacu captures included an 8.75-inch specimen pulled from a private pond in Delaware County (August 2000), a 2.7-pound pacu hooked in the St. Joseph River (July 2002), a 15-inch specimen bagged at Lake Shafer (August 2002), a 14-incher caught at Praxair Dam, in Porter County (August 2003), and a 15-inch specimen caught in a Johnson County gravel pit (date unknown).[28]

Yet another finny visitor from South America, the arawana (*Osteoglossum bicirrhosum*)—or Amazon monkey jumper—surfaced in Steuben County's Lake George, on 15 October 2001. While record specimens of arawana may approach three feet in length, tipping the scales at fifteen pounds, the Indiana specimen measured a mere twenty inches. Another arawana was pulled from Deep River, in Lake County, in September 2003.[29]

South American piranhas have been caught at several Indiana lakes and ponds. *Courtesy U. S. Fish and Wildlife Dept.*

More startling yet are the reports of bull sharks (*Carcharhinus leucas*) found in Indiana's freshwater lakes and rivers. Known worldwide, from Australia to South America, bull sharks—also known as river sharks and freshwater whalers—demonstrate a peculiar fondness for inland waters, with specimens sighted as far as 2,400 miles upstream in Brazil's Amazon. Transit of the Mississippi may explain two bull sharks seen near Evansville, in the Ohio River, but some human agency presumably deposited the specimen recovered from Lake Monroe. Bull sharks may reach eleven feet in length, and they are certified man-eaters, ranked on a par with tiger sharks by some experts, where risk to swimmers is concerned.[30]

Other foreign fish also appear in Indiana waters, but not on official lists of recognized exotics. In July 1995, DNR biologists netted a 5.9-inch bala shark (*Balantiocheilus melanopterus*) at Diamond Lake, in Noble County. (Despite its common name, this popular Asian aquarium fish is not a shark.) In 2001, a 9.9-inch tinfoil barb (*Barbus schwanefeldi*) was caught in Clay County's West Brazil Pond. Two Oriental weatherfish (*Misgurnus anguillicaudatus*) were hooked from the West Branch of the Grand Calumet River on November 4, 2002. Three months later, on January 27, 2003, a dead tiger oscar (*Astronotus ocellatus*) appeared on the bank of Blue Lake, in Whitley County. With the exception of free-swimming bull sharks, DNR spokesmen assume that all tropical fish found in Hoosier lakes and rivers are released deliberately by negligent owners tired of caring for their pets.[31]

The same cannot be said for eight species of exotic birds listed by state authorities. Foreign species ranked as abundant by the DNR include the European starling (*Sturnus vulgaris*), house sparrow (*Passer domesticus*), and rock dove (*Columba livia*). Others, rated rare, include the Eurasian collared dove (*Streptopelia decaocto*), Eurasian tree sparrow (*Passer montanus*), house finch (*Carpodacus mexicanus*), mute swan (*Cygnus olor*), and ring-necked pheasant (*Phasianus colchicus*). Howard Allison names the African cattle egret (*Bubulcus ibis*) as an exotic species "frequently reported in

Indiana," but DNR spokesmen disagree, listing it instead as a rare migratory species.[32]

On February 15, 2002, an even stranger bird appeared at Terry Beedle's home outside Bedford, Indiana. The emu (*Dromaius novaehollandiae*) is Earth's second-largest flightless bird, a native of Australia, whose adults may stand 6.5 feet tall and weigh 100 pounds, running at speeds of 40-50 miles per hour. The Bedford specimen measured 5.5 feet and showed no inclination to flee when offered food. Emus are often raised for slaughter on commercial farms in North America and elsewhere, but public searches for the owner of Beedle's visitor proved fruitless. Its point of origin remains unknown.[33]

Exotic mammals are less common in the Hoosier state, but DNR reports admit that two have made themselves at home. Both are Scandinavian rodents—Sweden's house mouse (*Mus musculus*) and the Norway rat (*Rattus norvegicus*)—which spread worldwide with human voyagers during the Age of Exploration. A larger species verified from Indiana, but thus far omitted from DNR listings of resident wildlife, is the wild boar (*Sus scrofa*), whose normal range extends from Europe and North Africa through southern Russia, into Southeast Asia. On December 25, 2000, coyote hunters David Lenning and Jesse Staggs surprised four large hogs and killed two of them near Buddha, in Lawrence County. Because the DNR regards wild boar as pests—albeit without recognizing their existence in the state—no license is required to hunt them. On the other hand, importing boar to Indiana is a Class D felony, with penalties including jail time and a $10,000 fine.[34]

Another strange and fatal encounter occurred near Columbia City (Whitley County) on October 1, 2004, when bowhunter Kevin Blum fired at an animal he thought to be a white-tailed buck. His aim was true, but his vision was faulty. Instead of a white-tail, Blum killed a much larger red deer (*Cervus elaphus elaphus*), native to Europe and the British Isles. Its nearest relative, the elk (*C. elaphus*), was extirpated by Hoosier hunters in 1839. As with the wild boar mentioned above, no penalties applied since DNR agents do not recognize red deer as a resident species. In fact, they described Blum's kill as "dandy." Red deer are raised specifically for "sport" in several parts of the United States, but no deer farmers could be found in the neighborhood of Blum's adventure.[35]

Bull sharks, while a marine species, sometimes swim far inland along freshwater rivers. *Courtesy U. S. Fish and Wildlife Dept.*

On November 29, 1903, the *Evansville Courier & Press* carried the following report of a strange beast captured in southwestern Indiana:

> Edward Smith of Long Branch is the possessor of a strange animal that was captured near his home yesterday. Dozens have seen it, but no one has been able to tell what it is. Smith said: "It is as big and ferocious as a tiger. Its head resembles that of a coon, but the rest of the body looks more like a dog. It is about 2 feet long, has a long, bushy tail and bright-red eyes." The strange animal will be brought to Evansville and placed on exhibition in a few days.[36]

The Evansville "tiger-dog" may have been a coatimundi. *Courtesy U. S. Fish and Wildlife Dept.*

While a two-foot-long tiger might be ferocious, it hardly qualifies as "big." In fact, Smith's description more closely resembles a South American coatimundi (*Nasua nasua*), like the one killed near Falls City, Nebraska, in 1968. Sadly, the specimen was not preserved or photographed, making positive identification impossible.[37]

In 1998, a Hoosier identified only as "Syrus" observed a strange mammal while hunting in Crawford County. It resembled a large mongoose (Family *Herpestidae*), but unlike that fearsome Old World predator, it "interacted" peacefully with a group of playful squirrels, prompting author Brad LaGrange to dub it the "King Squirrel." Coaxed by LaGrange, Syrus viewed photos of a coatimundi and excluded it as a prospect. LaGrange then suggested a mink (*Mustela vison*), while noting that minks—found statewide on an "occasional" basis—are also voracious carnivores. The creature remains unidentified, with no further sightings on file.[38]

What Else?

From this brief summary, it is apparent that the Hoosier State harbors a wide range of exotic and "hypothetical" species, both acknowledged and officially unrecognized by wildlife management authorities. As for *what else* awaits unwary campers, hikers, hunters, and zoologists in Indiana, subsequent chapters provide an overview of creatures even more unusual—and sometimes frightening—than those thus far examined.

A mink fits the description—but not the temperament—of Indiana's "king squirrel." *Courtesy U. S. Fish and Wildlife Dept.*

Chapter 2
RAMPANT REPTILES

Indiana wildlife officers recognize no exotics among the state's fifty-four identified reptile species, although three neighboring species (discussed in Chapter 1) are dubbed "hypothetical."[1] Despite that firm official stance, however, scaly visitors of unknown origin appear with startling regularity around the Hoosier State. Some hail from other parts of North America, while others trace their roots to distant jungles—and a few match no description known to modern science. We begin our tour of Indiana's cryptic crawlers with a group that frightens many humans most of all.

Snakes in the Grass

Officially, Indiana harbors thirty-one known and two hypothetical species of snakes. Four species—three of them considered rare and threatened by humans—are venomous. The rest are harmless, relatively small, and like all snakes around the world, provide a valuable service by consuming vermin.[2]

So says officialdom. And yet ...

For more than a century, reports of giant snakes have circulated through the Hoosier State. The oldest case with details presently available is that of "Big Jim," a ten-foot rattlesnake of unknown species nicknamed for a Knox County logger it allegedly killed in 1881. Over the next seventeen years, locals stalked Big Jim in vain and blamed the snake for many livestock deaths. Sullivan County farmer W. H. Thompson allegedly killed the rattler in 1908, when it invaded his pigpen. Its skin, stretched and mounted, supposedly measured twelve feet, while its rattle boasted twenty-nine segments.[3]

Midway between Big Jim's initial rampage and his ultimate demise, an even larger rattlesnake appeared in Scott County, eighty miles east of Knox. James Graham was collecting tree bark in spring 1891, when he stumbled on a nest of rattlers and killed ten large serpents, then spied an eleventh "which looked as large as all the balance." Devising a makeshift "lasso or harpoon," Graham killed the last snake, which allegedly measured nineteen feet long, with forty segments to its rattle. According to a newspaper report from May 1891, "the skin was stuffed and will be sent to a museum." What actually happened to the trophy after that remains unknown.[4]

Indiana authorities recognize two species of native rattlesnakes, the timber rattler (*Crotalus horridus*) and the eastern massassauga (*Sistrurus catenatus catenatus*), both of which are rare and threatened with extinction. The largest timber rattler on record measured 6 feet 2.5 inches long, while the record eastern massassauga was much smaller, at 3 feet 3.5 inches. Even the largest known rattler—the eastern diamondback (*Crotalus adamanteus*)—never officially exceeds eight feet in length. Snake skins may stretch up to 30 percent when tanned, but even so, a 12-foot mounted skin would still require a living snake some 8.5 feet long.[5]

Author George Eberhart claims further giant snake sightings from eight other Indiana counties—Adams, Allen, DuBois, Marion, Orange, Pike, Ripley, and Shelby—but he provides dates and details for only one case. On June 23, 1952, while driving with his family along Spy Run Creek in Fort Wayne (Allen County), D.A. Crance reportedly saw an eighteen-foot bluish-gray snake cross the highway in front of his car. The snake's head, Crance claimed, was as big as a bulldog's. Sheriff Harold Zeis led a fruitless three-day search for the serpent, nicknamed "Pete

The timber rattlesnake is Indiana's largest venomous snake. *Courtesy U. S. Fish and Wildlife Dept.*

the Python." Eberhart says that the incident ended on June 18 with a "hoax story" in the *Fort Wayne Journal-Gazette,* but my inquiry to that newspaper in April 2006 brought word that no giant snake tales remained on file. Likewise, inquiries to the seven other counties named by Eberhart failed to produce any substantiating details.[6]

There *are* pythons in modern Indiana, though. In mid-July 2001, a twelve-foot Burmese python (*Python molurus*) was caught in Brown County's Yellowwood State Forest. Bloomington resident Justin Posthuma claimed the snake days later, but could not explain how his escaped pet had traveled so far from home. Two years later, an eight-foot albino Burmese python appeared on the back porch of Bob Jones's home in Ellettsville, seven miles northwest of Bloomington. Animal control officers assumed the snake was another lost pet, but this time no owner came forward. On April 24, 2004, yet another albino Burmese python surfaced outside Decatur, frightening a hiker and his four children. Once again, police blamed some still-unknown owner for dumping the snake in the wild.[7]

While pythons may be common pets today, they were not readily available to Hoosier residents in August 1895, when a giant snake appeared in rural Jay County northeast of Muncie. Poultry dealer William James was talking business with two farmers when they heard "sounds of fence rails falling" and saw "a hugh [sic] reptile of the black snake species" emerge from the roadside grass. The snake tried to crawl under James's wagon, but proved too large to pass between its wheels, so it crawled around instead and vanished in the weeds. James and his companions, all too frightened to pursue the reptile, estimated that it measured twenty to forty feet long.[8]

Pythons are often sold as pets in the United States. *Courtesy PD Photo.org.*

Leaping Lizards

With rare exceptions, lizards evoke less fear and disgust from most humans than do snakes. Indiana boasts six native and one "hypothetical" species, ranging in maximum length from 2.75 inches (*Eumeces anthracinus*) to 11.25 inches (*Ophisaurus attenuatus*).[9] Once again, however, the natives are not alone.

In August 2001, multiple witnesses reported a five-foot-long monitor lizard (*Varanus* sp.) cavorting around Lake Lemon, in western Brown County. Sylvia and David Lewis filed the first report, followed by animal control officer John Houts, who failed to net the reptile. As with the state's several python sightings, authorities blamed a still-unidentified reptile collector for freeing the lizard, but their efforts to corral it failed. Winter presumably killed the lizard, whose various relatives hail from Africa, the Middle East, Southeast Asia, and Australia. Adult monitors commonly reach four to six feet in length, and one species—the fearsome Komodo dragon (*V. komodoensis*)—is Earth's largest known lizard, sometimes exceeding ten feet in length.[10]

The lost-pet theory makes sense in Indiana, although certain warmer states like Florida now boast breeding colonies of monitor lizards. A 3.5-foot green iguana (*Iguana iguana*) nearly joined the Hoosier cryptid list in July 1995, when it fled the home of owner Dorie Yorgen on Bloomington's south side. Fortunately, Yorgen quickly missed her pet—named "Aggie"—and found it hiding in a neighbor's tree. Even then, however, capturing Aggie was an arduous process, requiring negotiations with the fire department, animal control, and finally a private trapper. Had Yorgen been away from home or less attentive, Aggie may well have entered local legend.[11]

Monitor lizards have been seen, but never captured, in Indiana's forests. *Courtesy FreeStockPhotos.com.*

See Ya Later, Alligator

No reptile family of North America grows larger, or appears more out of place in Indiana, than the *Crocodylia*. Science recognizes three groups of crocodilians, including the alligators and caimans (Family *Alligatoridae*), the crocodiles (Family *Crocodylidae*), and the gharial (Family *Gavialidae*). Of twenty-two known species worldwide, only two—the American alligator (*Alligator mississippiensis*) and the American crocodile (*Crocodylus acutus*)—are native to the United States. An exotic visitor, South America's spectacled caiman (*Caiman crocodilus*), has also established breeding colonies in southern Florida. While the rare *C. acutus* normally appears only in far-southern Florida and on certain Caribbean islands, *A. mississippiensis* claims a broad range spanning all or part of ten states, from North Carolina westward through Arkansas, southeastern Oklahoma, and eastern Texas. Alligators once ranged farther north along the Mississippi River, but human encroachment drove them to the brink of extinction in several states, and their dramatic comeback in the late twentieth century does not include Indiana.[12]

Or, does it?

In fact, Indiana's first recorded sighting of a misplaced crocodilian dates from April 29, 1908. On that date, residents of Decker Township (Knox County) reported a "crocodile" living in a swamp on Henry Decker's farm. Neighbor Mathias Pickel described the beast's nocturnal bellows, but it gave the slip to hunters and escaped.[13]

Three years and one month later, on May 21, 1911, the state logged its second—and most unusual—crocodilian encounter. As explained in that day's *Los Angeles Times*: "During the hard rain here today an alligator two feet long fell from the clouds and, landing on the step of the home of Mrs. Hiram Winchell, tried to crawl in at the front door. The visitor was killed by Mrs. Winchell and several other women with bed slats."[14]

On December 31, 1946, the *Indianapolis Star* reported that two hunters, James Audaer and Ben Melvin, had killed an alligator in Mariah Creek, in Vincennes. Residents of Petersburg, eighteen miles to the southwest, claimed that the same reptile had dwelt in a nearby lake from 1900 to 1913, when a flood washed it into the Wabash River. From there, they suggested, the reptile "apparently worked up the Wabash into Mariah Creek." As author Brad LaGrange suggests, however, it seems hardly credible that any crocodilian could survive thirteen Indiana winters, much less forty-six.[15]

Another alligator sighting, reported by LaGrange without clear sources or dates, is sadly muddled beyond resolution—perhaps a garbled version of the April 1908 report. LaGrange says that a gator was seen by residents of Decker Chapel (in Knox County), and also "by passengers on the Big Four railroad as they crossed the Wabash at Francisville [sic]." Unfortunately, Francesville lies in western Pulaski County, some 175 miles north of Decker Chapel, and the Wabash River flows through neither county.[16]

Indianapolis, hosted several crocodilian visitors during the latter half of the twentieth century. The first, an eighteen-inch alligator, was captured at Fall Creek on September 9, 1959. Forty years later, in summer 1999, authorities pulled three gators from the White River and another from Fall Creek. The Fall Creek reptile, bagged on August 25, measured four feet long. Animal control officers told the *Indianapolis Star* that they believed two other gators were at large, one each in Fall Creek and the White River. All, they thought, had once been private pets, like the four-footer confiscated from a Bloomington resident on September 8, 1999.[17]

Hoosier crocodilian sightings and captures continue in the new millennium. July 2001 saw three alligators, each several feet long, hauled from the Wabash River in Huntington County. A private pond in Marion County yielded a four-foot-long caiman on June 30, 2002. Five weeks later, residents of Jasper saw (but failed to catch) another caiman less than half that size, paddling in the Patoka River. Parke County officers pulled an alligator from a rural creek on August 30, 2003, while others bagged a two-foot specimen at a retention pond in West Lafayette, on July 26, 2004. A thirty-inch alligator surfaced at South Bend, in the St. Joseph River, on June 2, 2005, and DNR agents shot it five days later. On August 9, 2005, officers dragged a fifty-pound gator from a mossy retention pond in Johnson County's White River Township. On May 27, 2006, two surprised fishermen caught a four-foot gator at a private lake in Marion County's Decatur Township.[18]

Thus concludes the tale of Indiana's cryptic crocodilians, as of press time for this volume, but we still have one cold-blooded visitor to meet. In some respects, it is the strangest of them all.

Authorities assume that alligators found in Indiana lakes are pets released by negligent owners. *Courtesy FreeStockPhotos.com.*

Chapter 3
OSCAR—THE BEAST OF 'BUSCO

Indiana's DNR recognizes sixteen native turtle species. One, the alligator snapper (*Macroclemys temminickiii*), is omitted by most guidebooks from their lists of Hoosier species, but state authorities place them in southwestern Indiana, where they rank as both rare and endangered. Alligator snappers are America's largest turtles, boasting a record shell-length of 31.5 inches. The largest known captive specimen weighed 251 pounds and lived for 51 years. A wild record specimen tipped the scales at 316 pounds.[1]

Neither of those giants lived in Indiana, but tales persist of an even larger specimen, sighted by various witnesses whose reports span more than half a century. Some called the giant turtle *Oscar*. Others know him as the *Beast of 'Busco*.

Was the Beast of 'Busco an alligator snapping turtle? *Courtesy U. S. Fish and Wildlife Dept.*

Early Stirrings

Churubusco, Indiana, lies eighteen miles north of Fort Wayne, in Allen County. According to local tradition, resident Oscar Fulk was first to sight the Beast of 'Busco, in 1898, swimming in a lake on his farm (later named Fulk Lake in his honor). One version of those long-ago events claims that Fulk carved his name on the turtle's shell—thus branding it "Oscar"—but no evidence exists of any nineteenth-century attempt to catch the reptile. Another sighting allegedly occurred in 1914, but no details of that incident survive today.[2]

On November 14, 1947, Fort Wayne resident Gale Harris purchased the farm from Fulk's granddaughter and her husband. Harris knew Oscar's story, but apparently paid little attention until July 27, 1948, when his brother-in-law, Ora Blue, went fishing on Fulk Lake with companion Charlie Wilson. The anglers returned with tales of "big waves a-rolling" and a huge turtle "going away like it was a submarine."[3]

A few months later, in early fall, Harris himself saw Oscar while helping his pastor—a full-time contractor named Reese—patch the roof of his (Harris's) barn. As later described in a June 1971 interview with author John Gutowski, Reese glanced toward Fulk Lake and pointed out some object "like a big head" cleaving the water. Harris and Reese ignored it that day, but a second sighting next morning prompted them to investigate. On reaching the lake, they saw a huge turtle, its shell approximately six feet long and four or five feet wide. Its head, said Harris, "looked as big as a baby's head." Thereafter, Harris saw the animal "more times than I can count," and once grabbed its tail while boating with his son. Thus provoked, Oscar capsized the boat, dumping Harris and his son into the water. Harris subsequently told the *Churubusco Truth* that when he latched onto Oscar, "[M]y hand wouldn't go around the tail."[4]

Hunting the Beast

With the spring thaw of March 1949, local newspapers mounted a hue and cry for Oscar. On March 7, the *Columbia City Commercial Mail* announced in its headline that, "Five Hundred Pound Turtle Would Make Lots of Good Turtle Soup." Three days later, the same paper reported that a hunting party of thirty or forty men had lassoed Oscar's hind leg with a chain, but the reptile escaped. The next day, a neighbor blamed Oscar for snatching his black Angus cattle, erecting a fence to prevent further raids. Then, on March 9, the *Truth* tired of its game, declaring that Oscar was henceforth "a dead issue as far as this paper is concerned."[5]

Undeterred by that turnaround, the *Fort Wayne Journal Gazette* published its first Oscar story on March 9, 1949, under the headline: "Busco's Behemoth Turtle (400 Pounds and 400 Years Old) Roams 10 Acre Lake." According to that article, an expedition from the Cincinnati Zoo had sighted Oscar sometime during winter 1948-49 and offered Harris $1,800 for the beast. A day later, the rival *Fort Wayne News Sentinel* pitched in with a headline reading: "The Tale of the Turtle Gets Top Billing: Production May Win Oscar." That article used "Oscar" as a nickname for the turtle, while *Journal Gazette* newsman Cliff Milnor apparently coined the name "Beast of 'Busco."[6]

All that ink inspired concerted efforts to locate and capture Oscar. After a sighting on March 12, 1949, local mechanic Kenny Leitch allegedly trapped the turtle in a makeshift pen, but it escaped before a mob of some five thousand spectators could catch a glimpse. Churubusco's Community Club appointed a Turtle Committee to study the problem on March 14, while Indiana's Society for the Prevention of Cruelty to Animals protested plans to harpoon Oscar. Woodrow Rigsby, a deep-sea diver from Fort Wayne, arrived to search Fulk Lake on March 18, but nearly drowned before an audience of 750 gawkers when his suit flooded.[7]

And so it went. Another diver, Walter Johnson, plunged into the lake on March 22, and sank in muck up to his chest. Tennessee brothers C.C. and R. V. Butler, advertised as professional turtle-trappers, pitched camp at Fulk Lake on April 4, then left in despair ten days later. Divers Johnson and Rigsby returned, but found nothing. Gale Harris allegedly netted Oscar on April 24, but the slippery beast escaped once more. A 225-pound female sea turtle, imported to seduce Oscar on May 9, failed to exert the proper allure. Frustrated hunters ditched their nets and dragged the lake with hooks, but all in vain.[8]

Public interest waned in June 1949, then flared anew on July 9, when Gale Harris allegedly harpooned Oscar, enjoying a brief thrill ride before the beast snapped his line. In fact, Harris now told the press, he had seen *two* giant turtles in Fulk Lake, swimming in tandem. On July 18, Walter Johnson claimed the last sighting on record, when Oscar supposedly raided a pen of live ducks used as bait. As usual, the turtle fled that trap uscathed.[9]

Frustrated and enraged by accusations of hoaxing, Gale Harris began draining Fulk Lake on September 14, 1949, pumping its water into a ditch feeding nearby White Lake. By September 22, he reduced the lake's size by 77 percent, from seven acres to two. September 29 witnessed the capture of a fifty-two-pound snapping turtle (*Chelydra serpentina*), lured to a trap baited with beef lungs, but Oscar remained elusive. On October 9, with Fulk Lake barely five feet deep, Harris claimed another successful harpooning—but once again, Oscar capsized his boat and escaped. Illness sidelined Harris in November, with the lake shrunken to sixty feet in diameter, and he finally abandoned the hunt on January 5, 1950, when a ruptured dam flooded the site with water previously pumped away.[10]

Two decades later, in his interview with John Gutowski, Harris voiced his belief that Oscar had escaped from Fulk Lake via "an underground current...that went to some other lake." Although perhaps farfetched, that explanation offers a possible explanation for another giant turtle sighting, reported from Black Oak Swamp (south of Gary, in Lake County) on July 14, 1950. County surveyors Samuel Brownstein and Henry Ewen were draining the swamp for conversion to farmland, when a turtle "as big as a beer barrel," sporting a head "as big as a human's," briefly clogged a nearby thirty-inch culvert. Ewen told the *Indianapolis News,* "I pushed on its shell, but man, when I saw the size of that thing, I knew I didn't want to tangle with it."[11]

Whether that was Oscar or *another* giant, it would not be seen again.

Hoaxes

As with many other cryptids, sensational publicity surrounding the Beast of 'Busco spawned various hoaxes and practical jokes. The first involved local pilots Ed Keckley and Carl Sheldon, who conducted charter tourist flights over Fulk Lake during the turtle hunt, charging passengers twenty-five cents apiece. As the excitement (and their extra income) faded, Keckley and Sheldon built a model of Oscar with logs and canvas, floated with an auto tire, in a bid to revive the excitement.[12]

Hoaxers used a sea turtle like this one to impersonate Oscar. *Courtesy U. S. Fish and Wildlife Dept.*

Several other hoaxes involved real turtles. On April 12, 1949, the *Indianapolis Star* revealed that the "Beast of 'Busco" displayed at a local grocery was, in fact, a leatherback sea turtle (*Dermochelys coriacea*) imported from Florida. A teacher from Indianapolis later admitted his plan to release the turtle in Fulk Lake, before he got "cold feet" and sold it to the grocer who had offered a reward for Oscar's capture. Seven months later, diver Woodrow Rigsby displayed a 100-pound alligator snapper in Fort Wayne, claiming he had hauled it from Blue Lake, west of Churubusco. Gale Harris branded the reptile a fake, whereupon Rigsby admitted purchasing it from an Arkansas zoo.[13]

Another hoax, this time involving trick photography, originated with the *Churubusco Truth* on April 7, 1949. That day's edition ran a composite photo of a massive turtle peering from the bed of a pickup truck, with a story that read:

> Four members of the *South Bend Journal*'s staff descended on Fulk Lake and in twenty-four minutes had captured the giant turtle with the aid of a radar set and a suction cup....The quartet of captors has planned to display their catch in the duck pond in South Bend's LaPere Park, but the problem arose as to the effect on the present inhabitants. However a Mishawaka insurance man discovered that his company wrote a policy insuring bodies of water with a "de-ducktable" clause.[14]

That tongue-in-cheek item prompted some 150 telephone calls to Gale Harris, seeking details of Oscar's capture, and prompted the *Truth* to run a follow-up story on April 28. That piece included another fake photo, depicting Oscar lashed to the bed of a semi trailer. It read:

> The largest turtle *ever* seen in these parts was photographed last week by Robert Lindsey near the Cincinnati Northern Depot with the water tower in view which provides a comparison showing the size of the turtle. This is the turtle that was in Fulk's Lake [*sic*] over in Indiana, which they had been trying to catch for weeks. The turtle ran out of food and came across country to Nettle Lake, where there are many fish.
>
> On the road between Blakesly and Eden the pavement has been dug out in one place where the turtle crossed in the night. And a motorist who was driving in that section had to slam on his brakes to avoid hitting the turtle. The turtle is known as "armadillacarnivoracarapace" scientifically, or "armadillarapace" for short. It always moves in the night and travels about 20 miles an hour. So it took about four hours to get from Fulk Lake to Nettle Lake, where it gorged itself. It ate so many fish there that it bloated and came to the surface and was noted by men working on the Emerson Werk's farm. They roped the turtle and hauled it to Bryan on

the truck as shown. It had been planned to transfer the turtle to a flat car and ship it to Chicago where it was learned from the fish and game warden that under section 1185964846873645-B of the game laws that it is unlawful to catch an armadillarapace between April 1 and June 15. The game warden agreed to permit them to cut the ropes that bound the armadillarapace and he was released about 11 o'clock at night.[15]

And so on. Another newspaper, the *Syracuse-Wawasee Journal*, claimed that "[t]he big turtle and his offspring have been seen in Wawasee and Syracuse lake [Elkhart County] many times during the last one hundred years. Catching the big turtles and shipping them to Chicago used to be a flourishing industry here. The last time this monster was seen here was two years ago when several people claimed to have sighted a 'monster' in Syracuse Lake."[16] Needless to say, no published stories from the 1840s or from 1947 verify those claims.

Turtle Days in 'Busco

While Oscar managed to elude all comers and (perhaps) escape to parts unknown, his spirit lives in Churubusco to the present day. In April 1950, eighteen local civic groups organized a General Turtle Day Committee, organizing a parade and festival which has become an annual event, including turtle races and election of a Turtle Queen. By 1971, Churubusco's summer Turtle Day was billed—no doubt, correctly—as "the world's greatest celebration for a turtle." Today, a sign outside the city limits heralds Churubusco as "Turtle Town USA.

While Oscar proved a boon to tourism in Churubusco, others sought to profit privately from his enduring legend. On June 26, 2002, the *Chicago Tribune* described the beast as "Indiana's Sasquatch in a Shell." Two weeks later, Indiana's DNR and the United States Department of Agriculture denied Churubusco resident Rusty Reed's petition to display "Crunch," a 165-pound alligator snapper, for "educational" purposes at traveling boat shows. Their grounds:

cold-blooded reptiles did not fit the legal definition of an "animal." Reed appealed that decision and lost the first round, on July 18, 2002, but state officials reversed themselves in November 2002, permitting Reed to take Crunch and three smaller turtles—all purchased from Georgia—on tour.[18]

Meanwhile, the mystery of Oscar, his identity and final where-abouts, remains unsolved. A large turtle shell labeled "Beast of Busco" hangs in the Two Brothers Restaurant in Decatur, Indiana, but canny observers agree that it is "most likely a fake."[19]

Chapter 4
PHANTOM COUGARS

With the exception of a few rare jaguars found in Arizona and New Mexico, America's largest wild cat is the cougar (*Puma concolor*)—also known in various locations as the mountain lion, puma, catamount, or panther. Once common from the wilds of Canada to South America, cougars supposedly were hunted to extinction in the eastern half of the United States between the mid-nineteenth and early twentieth centuries. Officially, the only recognized cougar population east of the Mississippi River consists of an endangered subspecies (*P. c. coryi*) clinging to life in the swamps of southwestern Florida. Another subspecies, the eastern cougar (*P. c. cougar*), is listed as extinct by most wildlife authorities. Indiana DNR spokesmen maintain that hunters killed the last Hoosier cougar 1851.[1]

Although officially extinct in Indiana since 1851, cougars still appear statewide today.
Courtesy FreeStockPhotos.com.

As in so many other cases, though, the experts seem to be mistaken.

John Lutz, founder of the Eastern Puma Research Network, based in West Virginia, reports eighty-one cougar sightings throughout Indiana, between 1965 and 2004, including eight cases wherein adult cats were seen with cubs in the wild. Harold Allison, writing in May 2004, asserted that his files contained 327 reports of "large cats that could be either a cougar...or of a black cat species unknown."[2] (For reports of "black panthers" and other mystery cats, see Chapter 5.) It comes as no surprise, perhaps, that cougar sightings have continued in the years since those reports were published.

Cat Tales

While limited space precludes listing of all Indiana cougar sightings, a few examples drawn from recent years suffice to put the riddle in perspective.

In July 2002, residents of South Bend, Indiana, worried that a cougar might be roaming the woodlands southwest of their city. Motorist Dorothy Gillen reported the creature, after it crossed a highway in front of her car. Local conservation officers suggested that the prowler might be a bobcat (*Lynx rufus*) or a coyote (*Canis latrans*), alternatives flatly rejected by Gillen.[3]

Ten months later, in May 2003, a more aggressive cat surfaced in Shelby County. Fairland resident Edra Ragland called police on May 9, to complain that a large unknown cat had attacked her parked car. Surprised officers found bite and claw marks, with muddy feline paw prints, all over the vehicle. Deputy Travis Maloney told reporters, "You could see where he hooked his top teeth into the top tread of the tire and sank his bottom teeth into the sidewall, flattening the tire." Tooth marks were also found where a section of the car's front bumper was dislodged. Police found bloodstains on the front of Ragland's vehicle, but if they were submitted for DNA testing, no report has yet been published.[4]

The year 2004 brought an increasing number of cougar reports. The *Indianapolis Star* noted two unconfirmed sightings in February, but provided no details. The same article also described (but did not publish) an alleged cougar photo snapped "around Christmas" 2003 by a motion-detector camera set in the Hoosier National Forest, southeast of Bloomington. Virgil Lyons, a friend of the photographer, told *Star* reporter George McLaren that he offered the photo to DNR agents, but "[t]hey don't even want to know about it. They implied it was probably a Great Dane dog." When pressed for a response, DNR spokesman John Marshall told McLaren, "I'm disappointed we can't confirm where [the photo] was taken."[5]

Two months later, another photo surfaced, this one depicting one of a hundred large paw prints found by Gunite Corporation workers at their plant in Elkhart County. This time the photo *was* published, with surprising results. Local resident Doris Ross saw the photo and identified it as a paw print from her 140-pound English mastiff, left on one of their tri-weekly walks near the Gunite facility.[6]

If that incident disheartened Hoosier cryptozoologists, Harold Allison soon boosted their spirits with an article published on May 2, 2004, offering selected details from his archive of 327 "big cat" reports. The list included sightings from six adjacent southern Indiana counties—Brown, Daviess, Jackson, Lawrence, Martin, and Monroe—with details of one cat seen mauling a deer, while others left droppings and claw marks on trees. Allison also described (but did not publish) "a very good picture" depicting a cougar at large in Brown County.[7]

Autumn 2004 shifted the scene of cougar sightings to northwestern Indiana. Reports began around nearby Lynwood, Illinois, in September, and soon spread to Indiana's Lake County, where Dyer resident Wanda Cox saw a cougar weighing seventy-five to eighty pounds in early October. Lynwood police declared themselves "95-percent certain" that a cougar was at large in the vicinity, but Indiana wildlife officers remained skeptical, blaming coyotes or large domestic cats. The phantom(s) moved eastward in December, where Hedy Kokido spotted a cougar in Shorewood Forest, west of Valparaiso. Speaking to the Munster *Times,* Lieutenant Jerry Shepherd denied rumors that the DNR released cougars to control the deer population, but acknowledged that, "We get complaints every year about cougar sightings."[8]

May Daze

May 2005 witnessed the Hoosier State's most intense cougar "flap" of recent years. The flurry of sightings began on Wednesday, May 4, when Marion County sheriff's deputies investigated reports of a cougar seen prowling the intersection of East Washington Street and German Church Road, on the east side of Indianapolis. DNR spokesman Russ Grunden told the *Indianapolis Star* that no trace of a cougar was found.[9]

That official denial briefly squelched cougar sightings in the state capital, but the following week brought fresh reports from Monroe County, fifty miles farther south. There, as reported by the Bloomington *Herald-Times* during May 11-14, various witnesses reported a cougar-like felid prowling and howling around Griffy Lake—the same place where fisherman Jack Goe caught his pacu in July 2001 (see Chapter 1). While some locals only heard the cat squalling, Bonnie Lucas reported a neighbor's geese and chicken slaughtered, while Tammy Gray found apparent cougar tracks (described as one inch deep and five to six inches wide) on her rural property. Two other witnesses, Betty Morrison and Fred Purdie, reported separate sightings of "a huge cat," four to five feet long, not counting its tail. DNR wildlife biologist Scott Johnson told reporters that he "can't tell much from any track more than a couple of days old." Another department spokesman, Dow Myers, described tracks found near the site of Morrison's encounter as "bigger than a cougar's," but they remain officially unidentified.[10]

My own two-part encounter with a cougar-sized mystery cat occurred while the Monroe County sightings were in progress. At 4:30 a.m. on May 6, an unseen predator snatched one of my house cats from the front porch of my home. One week later, almost to the minute, I heard another scuffling sound and rushed outside to find my largest cat, an eighteen-pounder resembling a Maine coon, pinned to the ground by a tawny felid roughly three times its size. The attacker fled at my approach, but almost casually, vanishing into the woods with a parting twitch of its long, slender tail. Its would-be prey survived the incident, albeit with a fractured jaw.

Sightings continued through that hectic month. At 1 a.m. on May 16, Laura Harding heard some heavy trespasser walking on the roof of her mobile home in Smithville, six miles south of Bloomington. Her dog "went nuts" when the prowler jumped down, leaving large four-toed paw prints—3 by 3.5 inches—in Harding's backyard. Publication of that report prompted witnesses Ricky Duke and Mark Snyder to reveal their separate sightings of cats with bodies three to four feet long, both dating from September or October 2004. Meanwhile, Laura Harding left meat scraps in her yard to entice the creature, reporting a nocturnal glimpse of "big brown eyes" on May 18.[11]

Monroe County sightings and rumors continued through May's final days. On May 24, Ellettsville resident Amado Abaya reported seeing a "dark yellow" cat, "bigger than a coyote," running along the shoreline of a small lake near his home. It took him two weeks to file the report, Abaya told reporter Kurt Van der Dussen, because "I thought it was my mind playing tricks on me." The same day Abaya's report went to press, rumors spread that a cougar had been captured outside Bloomington, but DNR spokesmen denied it.[12]

In Search Of...

July 2005 brought widely-scattered cougar reports from Elkhart County, on northern Indiana's Michigan border, and from Dearborn County, in the far southwest. In Goshen, Elkhart's county seat, Phyllis Poole described a large cat that hurdled her fence to eat bacon grease from a birdfeeder, leaving paw prints three times the size of those made by her 100-pound German shepherd. Publication of Poole's account on July 5 produced other reports from witnesses who preferred to remain anonymous. Thus frustrated, DNR spokesmen told the Goshen *Truth* that they possessed "no 'official' reports or evidence of big cats in northern Indiana."[13]

Weeks later, on July 29, the *Dearborn County Register* reported six cougar sightings by three residents of West Harrison, spanning the past twelve months. Restaurateur John Laverty's encounter dated from 2004, while the sighting logged by Helen White and her daughter was much more recent. Bill Reichling, an Ohio spokesman for the Eastern Puma Research Network, collected three more sightings, but "experts" remained skeptical. Paul Strasser, owner-operator of Dillsboro's Red Wolf Sanctuary, told reporter Denise Freitag, "Chances of it being an actual wild animal is [sic] slim to none." That statement failed to convince Monroe County witnesses who saw yet another on June 11, 2006.[14]

"Pet" cougars do exist in Indiana, such as the 120-pound female confiscated from Bloomington resident Brian Stidd on September 23, 1999, resulting in a $100 fine for illegal possession of a dangerous wild animal. And "tame" cougars sometimes escape, like the 150-pound specimen that leaped from licensed owner Gary Dutcher's car, in Fort Wayne, during its visit to a veterinarian on January 31, 2004. (Police shot and killed the cat, after several failed attempts to subdue it with a tranquilizer gun.)[15] But do such strays account for *all* the cougar sightings logged in Indiana?

Simply stated, it beggars belief that all 81 cougar sightings recorded by the Eastern Puma Research Network during 1965-2004, much less the 327 claimed by Harold Allison, arose from cases of exotic pets released by their owners. Certainly, the incidents involving adult cats with cubs suggest that cougars are breeding in the wild. A nod in that direction came from Washington, D.C., in 1973, when the United States Fish and Wildlife Service added "extinct" eastern cougars to the federal endangered species list. Much more recently, on April 7, 2006, Missouri's conservation commission officially removed cougars from the state's endangered list, citing fears for public safety behind their decision that the cats "should not be allowed to mount a comeback."[16]

Do wild cougars exist today in Indiana? Evidence suggests that they do—and furthermore, that they are not alone as feline predators. In fact, as we shall see, much more exotic cats are frequently described by Hoosier witnesses. And some of them may well be dangerous.

Sightings of adult cougars with cubs argue against the "escaped pet" theory in some cases. *Courtesy U. S. Fish and Wildlife Dept.*

Chapter 5
ALIEN BIG CATS

Cryptozoologists define an Alien Big Cat (ABC) as any large felid seen, caught, or killed far afield from its normal range. Thus, a leopard roaming wild in the United States would qualify, as would a cougar in Australia. Strictly speaking, though, despite their size, cougars are not "big cats." That term, in science, is reserved for members of the genus *Panthera*—jaguars, leopards, lions, snow leopards, and tigers—who possess a bony structure in their throats permitting them to roar. Cougars appearing where they are supposed to be extinct in North America are therefore *cryptids,* but they are not ABCs.[1]

That said, the Hoosier State has no shortage of ABC sightings, spanning some 130 years from the mid-nineteenth century to the present day.

We owe our earliest report to tireless researcher Mark Hall, who spent much of 1970 poring over back issues of various Indiana newspapers, including the *Richmond Palladium-Item* and *Sun-Telegram*. In those dusty archives, he uncovered the case of Mary Crane, mauled by a large, vicious cat in the Black Forest, near Rising Sun, in 1877. The predator left six-inch paw prints at the scene, but otherwise was not described in any useful detail.[2]

Three decades later, in 1908, residents of Gibson and Pike Counties, in southwestern Indiana, worried over sightings of a "panther" that disturbed the neighborhood. Hunters rallied to track the beast across a swamp, but treed and shot a hapless tramp instead.[3]

1948: "Year of the Varmint"

Four more decades elapsed before the next Hoosier ABC flap, inaugurating a fourteen-month rash of sightings christened the "Year of the Varmint" by authors Jerome Clark and Loren Coleman. The excitement began in July 1947, when residents of Fountain City (Wayne County) reported wild, unearthly screeching that frightened livestock in the night. Policeman Louis Danels saw a large cat of unknown species, while out for a Sunday drive with his family near Centerville. Danels described it as "the strangest, most vicious looking thing...[with] long front legs, a large head with small pointed ears, and small glittering eyes." According to Danels, "We all remarked that it was the most ferocious, evil-looking thing we ever had seen."[4]

A year later, in mid-July 1948, some unseen predator killed seven hogs on Dorten Moore's farm, southeast of Fountain City, eating only their hearts and livers. Moore called Sheriff Carl Sperling, who staked out the farm overnight with three deputies, but the prowler failed to return. Two nights later, neighbor Harold Erskine followed a "strange caterwauling noise" to Moore's farm, where together they found an eighth slaughtered pig. Another local farmer, Lewis Swain, heard a "strange whining call" on his land and found a flattened path through his wheat field "just like the one they found last year in the cornfield." Yet another farmer, unidentified by name, claimed that a creature barely glimpsed had chased him out of his own barn.[5]

On August 1, 1948, according to Clark and Coleman, conservation officer Charles Cornelius and game warden Clifford Fath met a large catlike animal "on the road between Quakertown and Roseburg." (Curiously, while Indiana has two towns named Roseburg—one each in Grant and Union Counties—there is no Quakertown. However, Quakertown *Marina* lies at the northern end of Brooksville Lake, not far from Union County's Roseburg.) Fath was driving when he saw a "varmint" sitting in the middle of the road and swerved to miss it. The beast, weighing an estimated 350 pounds, charged Fath's car and slammed into its side, then fled into the woods. The officers rallied a posse, tracking the animal with dogs, and while they treed it, firing into the leaves that obscured their vision, the creature escaped by leaping from tree to tree, out of range.[6]

Early on August 2, a farmer outside Liberty (the seat of Union County) found a 1,000-pound bull mauled to death near his home. Armed neighbors joined the hunt that afternoon, but they found only six-inch paw prints on the bank of Silver Creek. As described in the *Richmond Palladium-Item,* "Such tracks are not those of any of the wildlife living in this section of the country."[7]

On the evening of August 5, 1948, two married couples and their children—five persons, in all—were fishing in a pool below Elkhorn Falls (south of Richmond, in Wayne County), when a huge cat resembling a male lion (*Panthera leo*) menaced their party. One of the men ran to a nearby home and telephoned the sheriff's office. The cat was gone when Deputy Jack Witherby arrived, but he examined its tracks, which resembled "nothing I have *ever* seen before."[8]

The mystery deepened two days later, when teenage brothers Arthur and Howard Turner saw *two* ABCs at their farm, outside Richmond. The larger cat was brown, with a shaggy mane and "the appearance of a lion." Its smaller companion "had more the appearance of a panther and was black." Arthur Turner blazed away with a rifle, but the cats escaped, apparently unharmed. The beasts left tracks, but hunting dogs refused to follow them.[9]

The next day, August 8, farmers near Abdingdon sighted the same mismatched cats. Around 4:30 that afternoon, a "long black animal" crossed Robert Martin's property outside Middleboro, near the Ohio border. Hunters scoured the countryside in vain, reporting only that they had found five-toed tracks left by a creature weighing some 300 pounds.[10] (Most cats, including jaguars and tigers, have five toes on their front feet and four on the rear; cougars, leopards, and lions have four toes all around.)

On August 10, 1948, witnesses reported two lions lounging in a field near the Crane Naval Ammunition Depot, outside Bedford, 105 miles southwest of Richmond in Lawrence County. Commanders placed their Marines on alert, but the cats slipped away. Soon afterward, William Sterwalt lost a 400-pound calf at Gosport, forty miles farther north, in Owen County. A witness to that attack, Keith McGinnis, described the predator as "long in body, black in color, with short perked-up ears and a long tail." Another local, Eugene Myers, treed some screeching beast with his dogs, but could not see it through the thick foliage.[11]

The next day, James Leo found a huge cat sitting on the back porch of his home in Pennville, west of Richmond. He ran back inside for a knife to defend himself, but the beast was gone when he returned. Later that night, Robert Martin phoned police again, reporting that he had shot a "varmint" from his bedroom window. "I know I hit him," Martin said, "but I'm too scared to go out and see what I hit." Once again, officers dispatched to the scene found nothing.[12]

On August 12, Deputy Witherby and state conservation officer H. B. Cottingham led a 100-man posse in pursuit of Wayne County's persistent ABCs. They found tracks near a bridge, south of Richmond, identified by Cottingham as belonging to "some type of wildcat," but they admitted that tracks found near Abdingdon and Middleboro were "different" and much larger.[13]

Clark and Coleman report another ABC livestock raid on August 22, 1948, when farmer Orris Tate found one of his pigs fatally mauled near Sand Creek, surrounded by five-inch paw prints.[14] Unfortunately, the authors provide no more specific locators, and Indiana boasts a plethora of sites named Sand Creek. They include two widely separated streams in Hamilton and Porter Counties, the Sand Creek Woods (Hamilton County), two Sand Creek Townships (Bartholomew and Jennings Counties), plus a country club and campground (both at Chesterton, in Porter County).

Six days later, near Peppertown (Franklin County), "something" attacked Henry Forman Jr. while he was cutting tobacco on his farm. The animal ripped Forman's clothes and gashed one arm, then fled before he got a clear look at his assailant. That incident sparked more sightings of a large, "dark yellow" cat in the vicinity, but searchers returned empty-handed.[15]

Clark and Coleman place the Indiana "varmint's" last known appearance of 1948 on September 11, but they neglect to include its location. Witnesses Harry Rodenberg and Ed Raffe were repairing a roof at Rodenberg's farm when they glimpsed an unknown animal "about the size of a wolf and having yellow spots." It left without troubling the men or Rodenberg's livestock.[16]

That Old Black Magic

Black panther is a term devoid of scientific meaning. Strictly speaking, no such animals exist. The cats referred to by that name are usually leopards (*Panthera pardus*) or jaguars (*P. onca*), whose black coats result from melanism—an excess of melanin (dark pigment) in the skin. Despite some anecdotal evidence, no verified records of melanistic cougars, lions, or tigers (*P. tigris*) presently exist.[17]

That said, there is no end to "panther" sightings across North America, or in the Hoosier State. Between 1965 and 2004, the Eastern Puma Research Network logged 1,405 reports of black panthers seen in 27 states east of the Mississippi River. Twenty-seven of those sightings came from Indiana, but we possess details of only a few.[18]

According to authors Clark and Coleman, three witnesses on a farm near Noblesville (Hamilton County) saw a panther "five feet long and pitch black" in January 1951. The beast left tracks as large as "the palm of a woman's hand." David Simons fired at the beast but apparently missed, whereupon it "disappeared into a thicket along Stoney Creek." (In fact, Hamilton County has no Stoney Creek, though Henry County—fifteen miles due east—does have a Stoney Creek Township.) Coleman also reports "some black panther sightings" from Hancock County, in September and October 1962, but he provides no further details. Twelve years later, a hunter from Oriole (Perry County) allegedly wounded a panther five to six feet long, then tracked it in vain for two days before circling vultures convinced him to give up the search. Witnesses at Cloverdale saw another panther in 1983. Author Brad LaGrange reports a personal sighting from Leavenworth (Crawford County) in February 2001. Seven months later, in early September 2001, reports of a black panther prowling Elkhart County were eclipsed by the "9/11" terrorist attacks. Most recently, large black cats appeared near Unionville on June 16, 2006, and outside Bloomington seven days later.[19]

"Black panthers" are actually melanistic jaguars or leopards.
Courtesy William Rebsamen.

Lions at Large

While panthers roam the Hoosier State at will, lions have also put in several more appearances since the initial flap in 1948. Warrick County, in far-southwestern Indiana, logged reports of a lion at large in January 1958. In June 1962, three years before Monument City (Huntington County) was flooded to create the Salamonie Reservoir, local farmer Ed Moorman survived an attack by a cat which he and other witnesses described as an "African lioness." After two more sightings, Moorman summoned Sheriff Harry Walter, whose search party discovered nothing. On January 25, Moorman found ten of his pigs slaughtered, blood sucked from their necks, their hearts and livers eaten as at Fountain City, fourteen years before. Moorman called the sheriff again, but fresh searches proved fruitless. Other locals, jarred from sleep by "blood-curdling howls," theorized that a lion had escaped from some unnamed zoo or circus, but no big cats were logged as missing anywhere in the Midwest. Authors Clark and Coleman say Moorman was present, with other armed men, when the cat made its last (undated) appearance near Huntington, but two members of an Indianapolis TV crew jumped the gun—literally, in this case—and the beast escaped once more.[20]

Another rumored King of Beasts surfaced outside La Porte, far to the north, in August 1985. As in so many other ABC cases world-wide, authorities responded to the sightings but found nothing. No big cats were shot or captured. No zoos, circuses, or private owners of exotic animals admitted losing any lions anywhere in Indiana or environs.[21]

Lions also figure in several Indiana ABC reports. *Courtesy PD Photo.org.*

New Century, New ABCs

As we have seen, Hoosier ABC sightings did not end with the advent of a new millennium. At 6:30 a.m. on June 5, 2002, Sarah Burton stepped through the door of her home on Bloomington's east side and found an African serval (*Leptailurus serval*) sitting on her front porch. Though frightened by the two-foot-tall cat, Burton chased it away, then summoned animal control officers who trapped it after a protracted chase. Because the serval wore a collar, the "arresting" officers assumed it was a pet that had escaped, but no owner came forth to claim the animal. Rob Craig, director of Lafayette's Cougar Valley Farms cat sanctuary, told reporter Doug Wilson that while serval kittens cost an average of $2,000 each, incompetent owners often tire of the cats as they grow larger, cruelly releasing them to fend for themselves in the wild.[22]

An African serval was caught in Bloomington, in 2002.
Courtesy U. S. Fish and Wildlife Dept.

A larger ABC appeared in South Bend during late September 2003. Witnesses described the prowling felid as a typical "black panther," while other residents dismissed the sightings as a joke. DNR officer John Mortimore set traps for the cat, but failed to catch it.[23]

Five months later, Noble County witnesses reported another panther at large, around Albion. Those who saw the jet-black cat but failed to photograph or capture it included several law enforcement officers, a police dispatcher, and various civilian residents.[24]

May 2004 brought Harold Allison's report in the Bloomington *Herald-Times* that his files contained "more than 50 reports of big cats, both black and gray," from Crawford and Perry Counties. Later in May, during a phantom cougar flap in Monroe County, Bloomington resident Kristina Vosburgh saw a large black cat cross Tapp Road in front of her car. As described in her e-mail to the *Herald-Times:* "It was shaped and acted like a cougar. It was maybe as tall as 2-3 feet. It looked fairly young and muscular. It looked a lot like a cougar, but it was black.... I know it's almost impossible for a panther to be in Bloomington, but that's what it looked like."[25]

Six weeks later, in early July 2005, a witness identified only as "Melody" saw a sleek black cat in broad daylight, pacing along the roadside near her rural home in northern Indiana's Elkhart County. The cat was taller than her own black Labrador retriever, and had a long tail. She told the Goshen *Truth,* "It was completely black and sleek with no sign of a sagging belly. I chuckled to myself. I watched it for a few minutes until it strolled out of sight toward the woods. I was glad it stayed in the road and didn't veer from its path to bother the horses."[26]

Sherry Rohan, of Whitehall (Owen County), was less fortunate on January 31, 2006, when a black cat larger than her German shepherd invaded her pig pen, fatally mauling seven small porkers. Neighbor Rose Bastin told the Associated Press, "I've been hearing about it for a year or so. Panthers, mainly. You hear of people seeing it. It's not really strange to hear that." DNR spokesman remained skeptical, but Officer Angie Goldman admitted, "We would never say that they're not out there." Neither Sherry Rodman nor her husband Tony called authorities—"It wouldn't do no good," they said—but vowed to shoot the panther if it visited their farm again.[27]

Although Owen County's predator ignored that challenge, a new flap engulfed neighboring Monroe County in March 2006. An unseen mauler savaged three of Susan Pauly's dogs, killing an adult Labrador retriever, and while DNR investigators blamed coyotes or wild dogs, some locals named a different suspect. An employee of the Grandview Elementary School, residing near the Morgan-Monroe State Forest, tried to videotape "a large black panther" as it crossed her backyard, but her camera's dead batteries foiled the attempt. Advised of the sighting, DNR agent Dow Myers told reporter Kurt Van der Dussen, "It's very possible, but it's still unconfirmed. I wish I could get a good print or a good photo."[28]

Explaining ABCs

The quest for proof continues, while observers and cryptozoologists suggest potential explanations for Hoosier ABC sightings. Private owners are the first suspects, but as of press time for this book, no Hoosier individual or institution has been charged with accidentally or willfully releasing an exotic cat into the wild. The serval caught in Bloomington, complete with collar, proves that such events occur, but it remains the only ABC captured in Indiana, with its former owner still unidentified.

Speculation surrounding melanistic cougars persists as a solution for "black panther" sightings nationwide—but do such cats exist, in fact? Dr. Karl Shuker reports the "officially confirmed case" of a black cougar shot along Brazil's Carandahy River in 1843, but its skin was not preserved and the same region harbors melanistic jaguars. In North America, meanwhile, most official agencies deny the existence of black cougars, insisting that no such specimens have been confirmed either in the wild or in captivity. Most "panther" sightings, they suggest, result from misidentification of black domestic cats or dogs.[29]

A more novel solution, advanced by John Lutz in 2002, suggests that antebellum slave traders may have brought melanistic leopards home from Africa, along with their cargoes of human chattel, then released them on American soil to breed and expand their new domain. No documentary evidence exists to support Lutz's theory, but it finds a parallel in claims that United States military units may have released mascot cougars in Australia and England during World War II.[30]

Authors Mark Hall and Loren Coleman offer the most unusual—some say fantastic—explanation for lions and panthers reported throughout North America. They suggest that prehistoric cave lions

(*Panthera leo atrox*) did not become extinct during the Pleistocene ice age, some 20,000 years ago, but have survived to modern times in parts of the United States and Canada. Their theory explains both large, maned cats and smaller "panthers"—like the pair seen together by Hoosier witnesses in 1948—via sexual dimorphism, suggesting that some *P. l. atrox* females are black.[31] Fossil remains provide no clues to color for the ancient cats, and mainstream scientists predictably reject the notion of ice age survivors prowling the backwoods of twenty-first-century America.

Loren Coleman suggests that prehistoric cave lions may be responsible for some modern ABC reports. *Courtesy U. S. Fish and Wildlife Dept.*

Chapter 6
LAKE MONSTERS

Worldwide, more than 800 lakes and rivers have produced reports of unknown "monsters" swimming in their depths. Scotland's Loch Ness is the most famous, with reports of "Nessie" dating from the sixth century, but North America boasts some 41 percent of all lakes and rivers said to be inhabited by cryptids.[1] Renowned examples include "Champ" of Lake Champlain, and "Ogopogo" of Canada's Okanagan Lake.

And Indiana, as we now expect, harbors her share.

Author Betty Garner cites the earliest reports on record, dating from the "1800s+," but her account is sadly lacking in detail. She says merely that certain unnamed "pools, sinkholes, [and] rivers" were inhabited by "reptilian monsters [with] horns like buffalo," and leaves it at that, without supporting evidence.[2]

In the pages that follow, we shall examine monster reports from thirteen Indiana lakes, ponds, swamps, and rivers, logged between 1838 and 1983, in approximate chronological order. All available details are furnished, in hopes of identifying the creatures—or, at least, to facilitate further research.

Lake Manitou (1838-1983)

Lake Manitou, near Rochester in Fulton County, bore an evil reputation with local aborigines long before the first white settlers arrived. Its name, in fact, translates as "Devil's Lake" from the Pottawatomie language. According to native legend, a devil-snake named Meshekanabek inhabited the lake, along with several lesser serpents. After Meshekanabek devoured a cousin of the benevolent spirit Messou, Messou swore vengeance and disguised himself as a lakeside

Large serpentine creatures are reported from lakes around the world. *Courtesy William Rebsamen.*

tree stump, to stage an ambush. Meshekanabek and his minions saw through the ruse and attacked the stump, but Messou prevailed and killed Meshekanabek after a fierce battle. The fate of Meshekanabek's cronies is not recorded. Perhaps they remained in the lake.[3]

Fulton County's first white settlers heard the legend upon their arrival, in 1836, but they paid little attention until July 1838, when four local fishermen reported sightings of a creature "which they suppose to have measured 60 feet." Soon afterward, blacksmith John Lindsey rode along the lakefront and saw "some animal raise its head three or four feet above the water," two hundred feet offshore. The *Logansport Telegraph* (July 21) relayed Lindsey's account of the beast as follows: "The head he described as being about three feet across the frontal bone, and having something of the contour of a 'beef's head,' but the neck tapering, and having the character of the serpent; color dingy, and with bright yellow spots. It turned its head from side to side with an easy motion, in apparent survey of the surrounding objects."[4]

The *Telegraph* followed that report with another harking back to 1827. In that year, the newspaper said, pioneer surveyor Austin Morris complained that none of his flagmen would work near the water, for fear of a lake-dwelling "Indian terror." Historian Bruce Hess questions that account, suggesting that it may have been a "bandwagon" story designed to improve the *Telegraph*'s sales.[5]

Enter George Winter, a frontier wildlife artist who reached Indiana in 1837 and remained until his death, four decades later. Winter penned the *Telegraph*'s original story, describing John Lindsey's encounter at Lake Manitou, and he subsequently sketched the beast with "eyes as big as saucers and a forked tongue as red as blood." At Winter's urging, the *Telegraph* appealed to East Coast whalers for aid. "It is astonishing," the *Telegraph* proclaimed, "that such a small inland lake, so remote from the seas, should be as mysterious in its depths as in its legendary associations. But so it is. Boys! Up with your harpoons and to the Lake Man-i-too!"[6]

No harpooners answered that call, but the rival *Logansport Herald* still criticized the *Telegraph* for whipping up a *tempest in a teapot.*

In fact, the *Herald* noted, *Telegraph* reports of giant bones found near Lake Manitou were incorrect. According to the *Herald,* skeletal remains belonging to a woolly mammoth had been found at Cedar Lake (later renamed Bass Lake), twenty-five miles to the west, in Starke County. The *Telegraph* fired back with a demand to see those bones, chastising the *Herald* for its "pitiful and uncalled for thrust at an old ally and friend."[7]

No bones appeared, but the war of words continued into August 1838, before both sides apparently lost interest. Lake Manitou's monster lost face in the process, vanishing entirely for eleven years, until the story surfaced again in May 1849. On May 26, the *Logansport Journal* reported that fishermen in a "frail craft" had harpooned "a very remarkably large fish" at Lake Manitou. The fish measured seven feet long, they declared, but only its thirty-pound head with a startling duckbilled snout was preserved. According to the *Journal,* it was variously dubbed a paddle fish and a buffalo carp.[8]

In fact, those names describe two entirely different species, only one of which fits the *Journal's* description. The buffalo carp, or quillback (*Carpiodes cyprinus*), rarely grows beyond two feet in length, with the official record logged at twenty-six inches. It also has no duckbilled snout, as noted in the *Journal* article. Conversely, the Mississippi paddlefish (*Polydon spathula*) may reach seven feet long in rare cases, with weights exceeding 200 pounds—and it sports a "shovel" nose exactly as described. While sometimes called the spoonbill catfish, this primitive inhabitant of the Mississippi River system is not related to the catfish (Family *Ictaluridae*). Local historian Shirley Willard confirms that another paddlefish, weighing 116 pounds, was caught at Lake Manitou in 1888.[9]

Whether "the devil" had been snared or not remains a matter of debate in Fulton County, for Lake Manitou's monster reappeared in 1969. Carole Utter was fishing on the lake with her teenage son, when a "huge fish" surfaced near their boat. As she told me in May 2006, "The exact size I couldn't begin to imagine, but it was longer than our 14 ft. fishing boat, and we did not see all of it. My son wanted to chase after the direction it went, and I just screamed to get me back to shore." Utter's uncle, Phillip Krieg of Rochester, subsequently told her that "a number of people had seen it, some seasoned fishermen, who vowed never to fish on this lake again."[10]

Nor was that the creature's last appearance. Shirley Willard writes: "As recently as the 1970s the Manitou Monster has been seen and scared people half to death. But they do not tell the newspapers because people make fun of them and say they are crazy. However, they tell me because I believe them. There has been a big thing out there as big as a rowboat and it has been seen by too many people up close to be a figment of the imagination. So there has to be something, whether fish or monster or whatever."[11]

A full decade later, in spring 1983, Rochester resident Carol Young was walking to Coney Island, on Lake Manitou's western shore, when she experienced an eerie close encounter. "To my surprise," she wrote, in May 2006, "I saw a huge gray and pink something roll over in the water. It was 6 or 7 foot long, but I know I didn't see all of it. I shouted to our neighbor, and he just poo-pooed me. Then his wife came out and said she had seen the same thing. It's something you won't forget soon."[12]

Lake Manitou's "monster" may have been a Mississippi paddlefish. *Courtesy U. S. Fish and Wildlife Dept.*

Ripples Spread (1838)

Lake Manitou was not the only Hoosier lake supposed by aborigines to host a monster. Pottawatomie legends also placed another serpent in Starke County's Cedar (later Bass) Lake. Furthermore, the tribe believed that underground channels linked Lake Manitou to Lake Maxinkuckee, twelve miles to the northwest, in Marshall County.[13]

Is it coincidence, therefore, that monster sightings from Cedar Lake and Maxinkuckee followed the early reports from Lake Manitou in 1838? Were residents of Starke and Marshall Counties simply "piling on" in a bid for some local publicity? Culver librarian Jeff Kenney alludes to "one unique story of the monster appearing in Lake

Maxinkuckee that is *not* just a connection to the Manitou, in the late nineteenth century," but details remain elusive.[14]

Cedar/Bass Lake (1881-93)

In August 1893 an Ohio newspaper, the *Marion Daily Star*, described a series of monster encounters spanning twelve years at "Cedar Bass Lake." While no lake of that name ever existed in Indiana, Starke County's Cedar Lake *was* renamed Bass Lake in the early 1890s and bears no relation to the current Cedar Lake, farther west in Lake County.[15] Thus, the seeming mystery is solved—but what of the monster?

The first event reportedly occurred in 1881, when an undescribed monster ripped through August White's fishing net. Two years later, at Cedar Point (a real-life spot on Cedar Lake), "something swimming very fast near the surface" capsized a rowboat. Then, in summer 1892, passengers aboard the steamer *City of Kokomo* experienced an unscheduled thrill ride, when "something" fouled its anchor line and pulled the boat for several yards.[16]

The last and most dramatic incident supposedly occurred in May 1893, when four local luminaries went fishing on the lake. As named in the *Daily Star*, the fishermen included Sheriff Jacob Vanderweele, county auditor August Knosman (misspelled "Nosmin"), attorney (later circuit judge) George Beeman, and lawyer George Scoville, who defended President James Garfield's assassin at trial in 1881. Beeman hooked a fish, as he supposed, but was astounded when the unseen creature "gave them a free ride for half an hour." Finally, as it tired, Beeman and Nosmin began to reel in the 1,000-foot line. With only ten feet of line remaining, Beeman's catch surfaced, revealing itself as a greenish-black monster some forty feet long and three feet in diameter, "devoid of any fins," with a "huge and pointed" head. Turning to flee, it struck the boat with its tail, "smashing the stern into a thousand pieces and precipitating Beeman and Nosmin...into the water, where they were rescued with considerable difficulty."[17]

A Strange Menagerie (1889-92)

On February 21, 1889, the Vincennes *Western Sun* reported sightings of a fifteen-foot-long "whale" at Maucks Pond, a lake outside East Mount Carmel, in neighboring Gibson County. A century later, author Richard Day deemed the sightings "clearly absurd," the product of a journalistic tendency "to invent tales on slow news days," but even stranger stories followed.[18]

On April 22, 1892, the *Vincennes Commercial Weekly* headlined a report from local resident Isaac Daines, described in print as "a highly respected farmer whose veracity cannot be questioned." Daines claimed sightings of a sixty-foot serpentine beast in Horseshoe Pond, six miles south of Vincennes. Other witnesses included Daines's wife, hired hands, and neighbors.[19] As Daines described the animal:

> Its color is black on the back and sides. It inhabits the water and does not seem to venture any distance on shore. It glides through the waters of the pond with that easy and graceful movement peculiar to a snake swimming....When approached it becomes alarmed and swims away; if pursued it flees with wonderful rapidity.[20]

Daines claimed that he had tried to kill the serpent several times, but all in vain. His new plan, to recruit a firing squad of locals armed with Winchester repeating rifles, may have been communicated to the beast somehow, as it apparently decamped for parts unknown.[21]

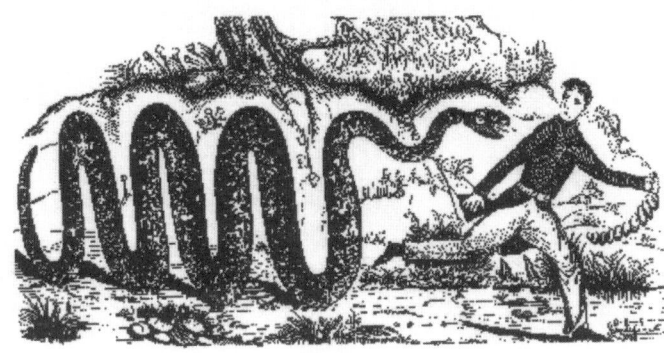

This illustration from a 19th-century Indiana newspaper depicts the beast of Horseshoe Pond as a huge rattlesnake. *Courtesy author's collection.*

Two months later, a rather different "sea serpent" surfaced in Big Swan Pond, four miles farther south. The new beast was smaller—only twenty to twenty-five feet long—with a white doglike head and white throat, carried well above the water's surface as it swam. Unlike its black neighbor from Horseshoe Pond, the Big Swan beast was "spotted or mottled, red and yellow, like the side of a large water snake." As usual, the witnesses who glimpsed it were "men of good repute for veracity." Unfortunately, by the time a hunt was organized, this serpent, too, had disappeared.[22]

Echoes of Manitou (1893-94)

Soon after the final report from "Cedar Bass Lake," three young women from Huntington—Eva Douglass, Cora Kilander, and Cora Nave—saw a strange beast in the Wabash River, near its western confluence with Huntington Lake. As reported in the press, the animal "appeared to be a huge sea serpent [sic]. Its head was above the water; its body submerged, but two or three feet of tail were above the water's surface, and it kept up a splashing with its tail, moving its head from side to side in serpentine manner." Its head, according to the witnesses, resembled a sea lion's, complete with whiskers, and was "as large as the head of a child 12 years old."[23]

The action shifted west again in 1894, this time to King Lake, outside Delong, in Fulton County. Historian Shirley Willard reports monster sightings from the lake that year, but details remain as evasive as the beast itself.[24] Considering King Lake's location, twelve miles northwest of Lake Manitou and five miles south of Lake Maxinkuckee, it may represent another outpost of the monster web surmised by Pottawatomie tribesmen—or another example of practical jokers at work.

A Swamp Beast (1904)

Converse, Indiana, lies in the far-southeastern corner of Miami County, near the junction of the Grant and Howard County lines. In August 1904, the *Miami County Sentinel* reported a strange creature dwelling in a local swamp, on the back end of Frem Pence's farm.

There, while picking wild raspberries, a neighbor and her daughters "were suddenly startled by a number of unearthly screams....Their dog emitted a few yelps, then tucked his tail between his legs and left the swamp on the dead run." The woman's husband, armed, returned to stalk the unseen beast, but found instead two lifeless hogs, presumably its victims.[25]

Two weeks later, another berry-picking party returned from the swamp with more tales of unearthly noises. According to the *Sentinel,* "One of the women makes the claim that she saw a big black object beyond a clump of bushes from which the blood-curdling noise came." That time, a posse scoured the marsh and came back empty-handed. It remains unclear today whether those incidents involved a water-dwelling cryptid or a creature like Bigfoot (see Chapter 9), but I include them here since no description clarifies the matter.[26]

Big Chapman Lake (1934)

Indiana's next freshwater cryptid report emerged from Big Chapman Lake, northeast of Warsaw in Kosciusko County, on August 16, 1934. Witness H. W. Scott was fishing from a boat when he saw a large head break the surface. Scott described the head as two feet wide, with "large cow-like eyes." A brief account in the *Indianapolis News* named Scott's wife and Mrs. George Barnwell as additional witnesses, but their accounts supplied no further details of the animal's appearance.[27]

"Norristown Nessie" (1930s-1950s)

The Flat Rock River, in Shelby County's Washington Township, produced its own rash of cryptid reports in the late 1930s, after global headlines heralded sightings of Scotland's Loch Ness monster. As a result, the Shelby County beast was dubbed "Norristown Nessie," and while some reporters view the episode as a hoax designed to increase circulation for the *Shelbyville Democrat,* it still deserves inclusion here.[28]

Suspicions of a hoax were unavoidable, since the first reports came from Elihu Miller, assistant circulation manager for the *Demo-*

crat. One morning at the office, Miller approached editor Norman Thurston—later general manager of the *Shelbyville News*—to say that his neighbors had seen a huge snake (or its tracks) on the Flat Rock's banks, north of Norristown. Thurston ran a short article on the creature and wired it on to the *Indianapolis News,* which reprinted the piece and requested more details. Miller pitched in with a series of stories describing more sightings around Norristown.[29]

As reported in the *Democrat,* witnesses offered diverse descriptions of the beast. Some portrayed a huge snake crawling over dry land, while others described an apparent mammal or a huge amphibian paddling in the river. Fleeting glimpses were the norm, and many of the *Democrat's* reports were clearly tongue-in-cheek. Still, Norman Thurston would recall the flap in later years as "the biggest story ever to hit the Norristown area."[30]

It was so big, in fact, that search parties rallied and took to the field in pursuit of the beast, all in vain. According to journalist Ron Hamilton, Elihu Miller later confessed that some unnamed Norristown resident had fabricated the monster's tracks by dragging sacks filled with dirt along the Flat Rock's banks. A strange epilogue from the mid-1950s involved sightings of an unknown creature swimming across the Flat Rock near State Road 9, with only its head breaking water.[31]

Hollow Block Lake (1960)

On August 5, 1960, five fishermen reported an encounter with a "square monster" at Hollow Block Lake, near Portland, in Jay County. Aside from its peculiar shape, the creature was approximately seven feet long and produced frightening screams. Mayor Ray Burk of Portland told the *Cincinnati Inquirer* that he "felt sure" the beast was in fact a drowned Holstein calf weighing fifty pounds, that was dredged from the lake near the same location. Witness Carl Gierhart refuted that claim, telling reporters he was "positive" the thing he saw was neither dead nor bovine. More than 100 locals, some armed with shotguns, prowled the lake's shore in search of clues but found nothing. Divers volunteered to search the lake bottom, but Portland officials declined. Nonetheless, swimmers and fishermen were banned from the lake for the rest of the week.[32]

Eagle Creek

Our last report, if so it may be dignified, includes no details whatsoever and may well be a mistake. Authors Loren Coleman and John Kirk include Eagle Creek, in Lake County, on published lists of supposed monster habitats, but neither source provides any dates or details of sightings. Meanwhile, Katie Sullivan's excellent website on aquatic cryptids omits Eagle Creek, but lists Eagle Lake (northwest of Fort Wayne, in Noble County) as a source of unspecified sightings. That confusion is compounded by vague monster reports from California's Eagle Lake, near Sacramento. Since my inquiries to Lake and Noble Counties elicited no answers, the confusion remains unresolved.[33]

Chapter 7
TENTACLES

Cephalopods (Class *Cephalopoda,* literally "head-foot") are mollusks characterized by arms or tentacles attached to their heads. Science recognizes some 800 living species, including cuttlefish, nautiluses, octopuses, spirulas, and squids. The giant squid (*Architeuthis dux*) is the largest known invertebrate on Earth, while the smallest cephalopod—the pygmy cuttlefish (*Idiosepius pygmaeus*)—rarely exceeds three-quarters of an inch in length.[1]

While most cephalopods have eight or ten arms, some nautiluses may have ninety. Cephalopods swim by a kind of jet propulsion, squirting water from the body cavity (or mantle) to propel them backward at high rates of speed. When unable to escape, many defend themselves with blasts of ink that cloud the water and repel potential predators.[2]

Without exception, all known cephalopods are marine animals, existing solely in salt water from the poles to tropic regions, but a few have found their way to Indiana under circumstances that remain mysterious.

Freshwater Octopuses

Indiana's Falls of the Ohio State Park is located at Clarksville, across the Ohio River from Louisville, Kentucky. It is part of the larger Falls of the Ohio National Wildlife Conservation Area. The park's main feature consists of fossil beds dating from the Devonian period of the Paleozoic era, ending 354 million years ago.

On November 21, 1999, tourists found a small octopus lying beached on the park's fossil bed. Park employee Paul McLean subsequently told investigator Brad LaGrange that the octopus "was not alive and it was not in a state of decomposition. It probably weighed less than a pound." Dominic Foster, supervisor of the park's aquarium, identified the specimen as an Atlantic octopus (*Octopus vulgaris*), but while Foster created a special exhibit to commemorate the discovery, he did not preserve the octopus itself. John Forsythe, a researcher at the National Resource Center for Cephalopods, examined photos of the creature and opined that it was either a Caribbean armstripe octopus (*O. burryi*) or a bumblebee two-stripe octopus (*O. filosus*).[3]

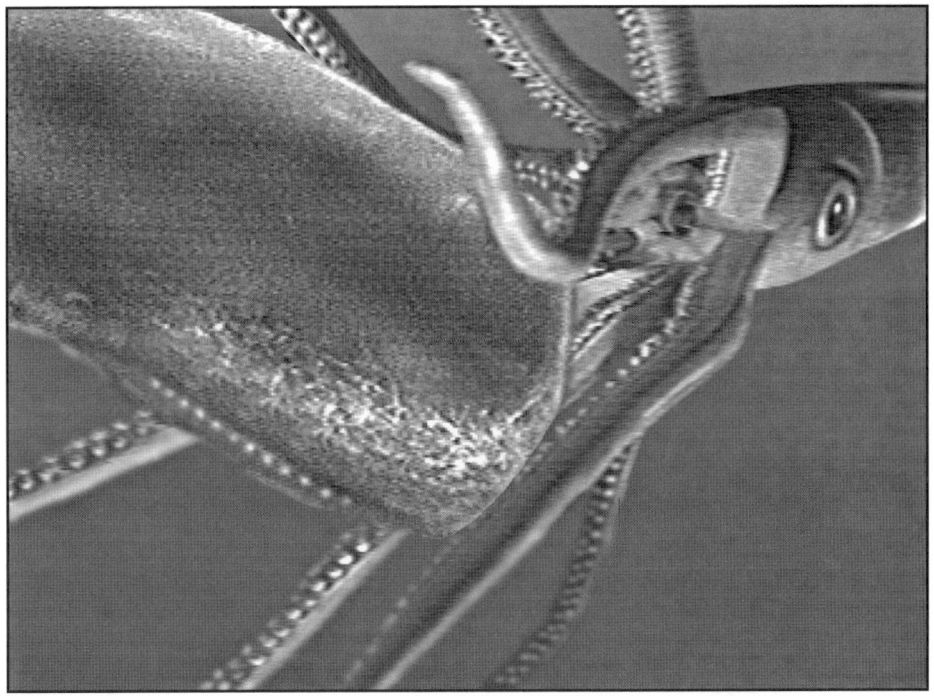

The giant squid is Earth's largest known invertebrate. *Courtesy William Rebsamen.*

Assuming that Forsythe was correct on either count, how did an ocean-dwelling specimen from the eastern seaboard or Caribbean find its way to the bank of the Ohio River? Forsythe notes that both *O. burryi* and *O. filosus* have been sold in the United States aquarium trade from various foreign suppliers.[4] Presumably, the owner of an octopus may have released it into the river, where it was sure to die, or else may have discarded it on shore during a visit to the park. The latter prospect seems improbable, but it is still more likely than an octopus surviving in fresh water.

Or, is it?

Before abandoning the hapless Clarksville specimen, we should note that it is not unique. In 1954, four boys pulled a live octopus with two-foot tentacles from a creek near Grafton, West Virginia, but it died soon afterward. Five years later, in January 1959, witnesses claimed a live octopus sighting from the Licking River, at Covington, Kentucky. Around the same time, another octopus was reportedly seen in the Ohio River, near Fort Thomas, Kentucky.[5]

After reviewing the slim evidence, authors Chad Arment and Brad LaGrange conclude that the existence of a freshwater octopus species "does not appear to be biologically impossible; merely biologically improbable." In defense of that view, they cite evidence that aging octopuses experience senescence, a state resembling human senility, wherein they stop eating and wander far from their normal habitats—perhaps farther afield than mainstream scientists are ready to admit.[6]

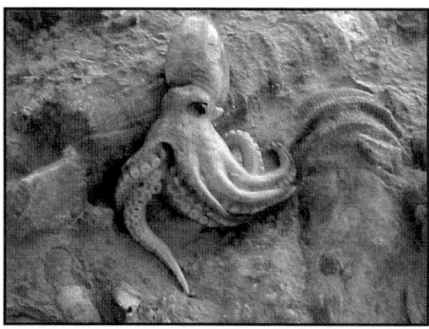

Paul McLean took this photo of an octopus found at Falls of the Ohio State Park in 1999. *Courtesy Paul McLean.*

Oil Pit Squids

If freshwater cephalopods in the Hoosier State seem unlikely, what should we think of squid-like creatures living in a pit of toxic sludge? The very notion seems preposterous. And yet ...

The auto industry once played a vital role in the economy of Anderson, Indiana, dubbed "Pittsburgh on White River" for its thriving factories. By the early 1990s, though, Detroit had fallen on hard times and many of the local plants were closed. One that survived was General Motors Corporation's Plant No. 9, Delphi Interior and Lighting, which manufactured various auto components including lights, plastic grilles, and soft bumpers.[7]

On November 15, 1996, while cleaning out one of the Delphi plant's several "sludge" pits, employees spotted reddish-colored squid-like creatures swimming in the lethal mix of antifreeze, oil, stripper, and Polyal (a chemical used to produce plastic bumpers). One thirty-year GMC veteran, who requested anonymity, later told *Anderson Herald Bulletin* reporter Ken de la Bastide, "The pit was full of these things, all swimming around. These were definitely living animals." They measured six to eight inches long, sporting tentacles "and possibly eyes." The startled witnesses caught one of the creatures in a jar and placed it in the plant office before returning to work.[8]

There the matter rested until March 1997, when the Indiana Department of Environmental Management (IDEM) received an anonymous complaint of "illegal hazardous waste activity" at Delphi Plant No. 9. The complaint included allegations of open waste containers, toxic waste buried beneath a new walking trail, and "unusual growth in a used oil pit." Ken de la Bastide headlined the complaint on March 4, then broke the story of the oil pit "squids" the following day. An IDEM internal memo confirmed that some "creature of unknown origin or type" had been found at Plant No. 9.[9]

The story took another turn, however, when IDEM inspectors visited the Delphi factory on March 7, and again five days later. By that time, no creatures remained in the sludge pit, and the captive specimen had vanished along with its jar from the factory office, apparently stolen. Sharon Morton, speaking for GM's management in Detroit, claimed the employees had found a simple bacterial growth in November 1996. "They described it," she said, "as the type of bacteria that would form when organic matter is placed in fresh water. They consider it harmless." When the sample disappeared, Morton said, Delphi staffers followed "normal security procedures" for a theft, then dropped the matter when no leads were found."[10]

Tamara Ohl, a spokesperson for the Environmental Protection Agency (EPA), told Ken de la Bastide, "They [GMC] did find something in one of the pits. They collected it and were going to have it sent off and tested to confirm what it was. But the sample disappeared. When they clean that pit, if GM finds something, they will take another sample and have it tested. They also want to find out what it was." Ohl, who had never seen anything similar in her EPA career, added, "I'm curious about it."[11]

Alas, that curiosity was never satisfied. The final clean-up at Plant 9 revealed no squids and no giant bacteria. While rumors of a cover-up persist, the mystery remains unsolved.[12]

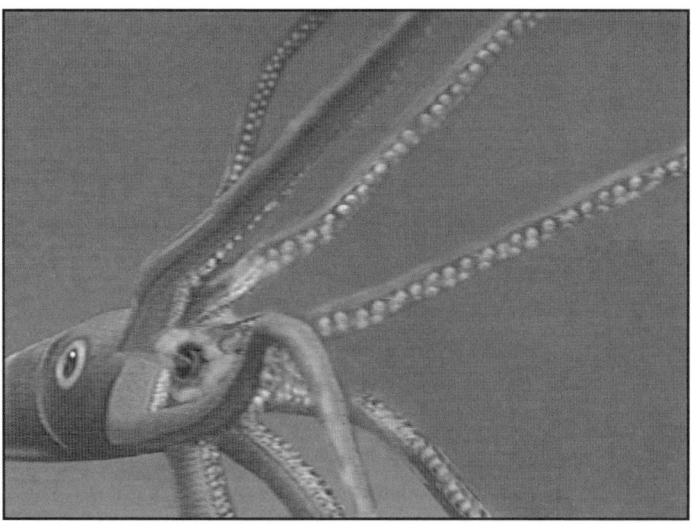

No trace remains of the squid-like creatures found in an Indiana oil pit in 1996. *Courtesy William Rebsamen.*

Chapter 8
KANGAROOS, DEVIL MONKEYS, AND NAPEs

Kangaroos and wallabies (Genus *Macropus*) are marsupials native to Australia, New Zealand, and Papua New Guinea. Outside their normal range, these easily-recognized animals also reside in many zoos and wildlife parks. Additionally, small breeding colonies of wallabies exist in the United Kingdom, imported and released by thoughtless private parties through the 1970s. No kangaroos or wallabies are acknowledged as living wild in North America, but that has not stopped them from appearing in various states since 1899.[1] At press time for this volume, Indiana had experienced two widely-separated kangaroo "flaps," which in turn have inspired some surprising explanations.

Round One (1974)

The Hoosier State's first kangaroo at large appeared at Rensselaer (Jasper County) in November 1974, six days after a two-week rash of similar reports from nearby Illinois and Michigan. At 8:30 a.m. on November 12, Alfred Hentschel saw a kangaroo emerge from a cornfield on the southern edge of town, cross Charles Street, and vanish into another cornfield. At noon, Charles James observed a 'roo from 300 yards, hopping in the woods near St. Joseph's College. Police responded to that call, but found no runaway marsupial. At 5 p.m., contractor Bill Babcock watched the 'roo hop past his office, toward a nearby gravel pit.[2]

Sightings resumed in Illinois on November 15, but the elusive leaper still had unfinished business in Indiana. Two days later, on a Sunday morning, Amos Miller, his wife, and two other witnesses saw a kangaroo while driving to church in Carmel, two miles north of Indianapolis. The creature sat beside Cool Creek Bridge, at Keystone and State Highway 234. Before day's end, a second Carmel sighting was reported. Police sought the kangaroo in vain, then told reporters, "We don't doubt the story one bit."[3]

The Hoosier flap ended on November 25, 1974, when farmer Donald Johnson saw a kangaroo outside Sheridan, twelve miles north of Carmel. Johnson was driving along a rural highway when he saw the 'roo "running on all four feet down the middle of the road." As Johnson drew nearer, the animal hopped over a barbed-wire fence, crossed a roadside field, and vanished in the woods.[4]

Kangaroos have been sighted throughout the American Mid-west, including Indiana. *Courtesy U. S. Fish and Wildlife Dept.*

Round Two (2005)

Thirty-three years elapsed before Indiana's next reported kangaroo sightings, in June 2005. This time, the flap occurred around South Bend, near the Michigan border. While working near the corner of Bendix and Boland Drives on June 27, tree-trimmer Walt Temple saw "something hopping, literally hopping from the center of the street to a hidden area and I thought, that must be a deer, but why is he up on two legs? It then hopped, hopped, hopped and disappeared and I thought, nah, it can't be a kangaroo." Instead, Temple explained, "I thought, 'It's gotta be a deer, it's gotta be a deer. But then why would it be on its back legs?'"[5]

Why, indeed? Animal control officer Sumyr Springfield answered Temple's call, openly skeptical until she saw the three-foot-tall beast for herself. Reinforcements soon arrived, and while reporting the discovery of "what they think is a bed for some type of animal," they failed to glimpse the 'roo again. Department spokesmen first opined that an animal in transit might have escaped from the South Bend Regional Airport, but airport official Michael Guljas quickly laid that theory to rest. Likewise, keepers at the nearby Potawatomi Zoo reported all their kangaroos and wallabies present and accounted for.[6]

Thus stymied, South Bend animal control officially called off its kangaroo hunt on July 13, 2005. Spokesperson Tammy Roberts told the *South Bend Tribune,* "Until we get another call, we don't have anything to go on." Not that there was any doubt about the animal's identity, however. Roberts added, "Our officer identified it. We know the difference between a deer and a kangaroo. We're 100 percent that it was [a kangaroo]." As for its prospects, Roberts said, "We know it would survive out there."[7]

The Devil Monkey Option

One longtime student of the phantom 'roo phenomenon who doubts that verdict, in at least some cases, is cryptozoologist Loren Coleman. Theorizing in conjunction with researchers Chad Arment and Mark Hall, Coleman suggests that some North American kangaroo sightings involve a species of unclassified primates resembling baboons, which he dubs "devil monkeys." One such creature, reported in spring 1973 from the neighborhood of Enfield, Illinois, drew tele-journalists from Kokomo, Indiana, to join in the hunt. Rick Rainbow, news director of Kokomo's WWKI-TV, allegedly sighted the creature on May 6, describing it as gray and stoop-shouldered, around five feet six inches tall. While Rainbow failed to catch the beast on videotape, he did secure an audio recording of its high-pitched cry.[8]

If Midwestern devil monkeys do exist, what could they be? One pos-sibility, and the most logical (if we ignore descriptions of the creatures seen by witnesses), involves pet monkeys turned feral after they escape from, or are released by, negligent private owners. Florida wildlife of-ficials freely admit that rhesus monkeys (*Macaca mulatta*) and squirrel monkeys (*Saimiri sciureus*) have established breeding colonies in the Sunshine State, and Coleman alludes to a rhesus that allegedly survived ten of Indiana's freezing winters. Chad Arment suggests that modern American may harbor relict specimens of *Protopithecus brasiliensis*, a Brazilian spider monkey of the Late Pliocene, that was twice as large as modern spider monkeys (*Arteles* sp.). Mark Hall nominates another prehistoric primate, the East African baboon, *Theropithecus oswaldi*, presumed extinct since the Middle Pleistocene.[9]

Mainstream scientists counter such theories with the argument that (a) both *P. brasiliensis* and *T. oswaldi* are in fact extinct, and (b) no evidence exists suggesting that either species ever set foot on North American soil. As for smaller monkeys of known living species, confu-sion with a full-grown kangaroo or wallaby seems unlikely.

Loren Coleman believes some witnesses mistake "devil monkeys" like this one for kangaroos. *Courtesy William Rebsamen.*

The NAPEs

Loren Coleman's "devil monkey" theory dovetails with that of another cryptic primate species which he has christened the North American Ape (NAPE, for short). Coleman coined the name to describe a group of large unknown animals that differ in certain critical respects from the classic Bigfoot or Sasquatch (see Chapter 9). Specifically, NAPEs leave apelike footprints—with an opposed big toe, resembling the thumb on a human hand—while Sasquatch and company are known for oversized humanoid tracks (hence the "Bigfoot" nickname).[10]

While Coleman claims no Hoosier NAPE sightings, Richard Eberhart cites four, reportedly occurring in Boone, Harrison, and Monroe Counties. That roster is deceptive, though, since two of the four locations listed—Lake Monroe and the Hardin Ridge Recreation Area—relate to a single incident from January 2002. And that case, in turn, presents no classic NAPE symptoms: indeed, the creature's four-by-five-inch tracks revealed only four toes. Since Eberhart provides no dates or details for the Boone or Harrison County sightings, we cannot evaluate those listings, but three unknown primate reports on file from those districts clearly have more in common with Sasquatch than with NAPEs (see Chapter 9).[11]

On balance, if monkeys seem unlikely to stand in for kangaroos, NAPEs and/or Sasquatch bear even less resemblance to marsupials from down under. The great, still-unidentified primates typically have flat faces, stand six to nine or ten feet tall, walk without hopping, and have no visible tails—in short, they are the very antithesis of kangaroos and wallabies.

That said, however, we should not suppose that Indiana's fields and forests offer only room enough for one cryptid. As we shall see, the Hoosier State is large enough for several—and all of them insist on showing up where they are least expected.

The North American Apes proposed by Loren Coleman bear little resemblance to Australian marsupials. *Courtesy William Rebsamen.*

Chapter 9
BIGFOOT

Throughout recorded history, every continent on Earth, except Antarctica, has spawned reports of large primates or apelike hominids unrecognized by science. They are known by many names around the world—as Yeti in the Himalayas, Yeren in China, Yowie in Australia, Almas in Eurasia, the Tano Giant in Africa, Bigfoot or Sasquatch in North America. And while a majority of Bigfoot sightings emanate from the Pacific Northwest, reports have been filed nationwide. In fact, of all the continental United States, only Rhode Island has no cases presently on file.

At press time for this volume, Indiana's Bigfoot roster includes 145 specific reports, plus an uncertain number of vague accounts referring to "several" or "multiple" incidents. Hoosier sightings span 167 years, from 1839 to 2006. A total of 135 reports occur in 54 of Indiana's 92 counties, while 10 others describe no specific location. Ninety-eight reports include actual sightings of unknown primates in the flesh, while 47 involve mysterious footprints, vocalizations, or foul odors commonly associated with such creatures.[1]

The Nineteenth Century

Indiana's first report of an unknown primate dates from December 1839, when settlers around Fish Lake (La Porte County) glimpsed a "wild child" at large in the vicinity. According to the *Michigan City Gazette:* "It is reported to be about four feet high, and covered with a coat of light chestnut-colored hair. It runs with great velocity, and when pursued, as has often been the case, it sets up the most frightening and hideous yells, and seems to make efforts at speaking." It also swam in the lake, while "whining most piteously."[2]

Artist's conception of Bigfoot, based on eyewitness descriptions. *Courtesy William Rebsamen.*

Four decades elapsed before the next sighting, near Lafayette, in July 1883. Mrs. Frank Coffman, a local farmer's wife, was passing through the woods when she saw a strange creature eating sassafras bark. It was "female in contour, with long black hair blowing in the wind. Short gray hair covered its body." A 100-man hunting party pursued the thing for half a mile, during which "[h]er feet touched the ground but seldom. She would grab the underbrush with her long, bony hands, and swing from bush to bush and limb to limb, with wonderful ease." Finally, the animal reached a swamp, where it "disappeared as suddenly and as effectively as an extinguishing light."[3]

Sometime in 1895, witnesses observed a mysterious creature inhabiting the woods near Sailor, located somewhere northwest of Indianapolis. (The town no longer exists, and proved untraceable.) The first public report occurred on May 1,1897, one day after farmers Adam Gardner and Ed Swinehart fired shots at a bipedal creature which "had every appearance of a man, save the body was covered with hair." It escaped with "rabbit-like bounds," although Gardner thought it was wounded. Search parties failed to locate the creature.[4]

1949-53

Another half-century separates the Sailor incidents from Indiana's next reported Bigfoot sighting at Thorntown (Boone County), in mid-July 1949. More than two dozen local residents saw the "big hairy beast," describing it as "a gorilla" with brown hair and protruding teeth. Fishermen George Coffman and Charles Jones got the closest look on July 14, when the animal chased them through Sugar Creek Township.[5]

Four years later, in summer 1953, a group of eight or nine witnesses met Bigfoot near Winamac, in Pulaski County. They described the beast as seven feet tall, covered from head to foot with long, dark hair, and walking on two legs. Several children claimed that the creature had only one eye. A male witness grabbed his rifle, but refused to fire because he was "afraid I might be shooting a man."[6]

Indiana Bigfoot sightings sometimes include multiple apelike creatures.
Courtesy William Rebsamen.

The 1960s

This decade produced ten specific reports from as many Indiana counties, including Carroll, Fountain, Jefferson, Ohio, Orange, Parke, Plymouth, Pulaski, and Wayne. Author John Keel also records five sightings from the fringes of the southern Indiana's Hoosier National Forest "pre-1970," but he offers no specific dates. Those sightings allegedly occurred in Dubois, Lawrence, and Martin Counties, with the last at "Burn City" (found on no current Indiana maps).[7]

While one of the specific 1960s reports involved only sixteen-inch humanoid footprints, and another concerned shrieks in the night like "the sound of a great cat," the remainder included eyewitness sightings of large unknown primates. Several of the sightings involved multiple witnesses. The creatures ranged from five to ten feet in height (the former described as "monkey looking"), and two of them left humanoid tracks in Jefferson and Parke Counties (1962 and 1966, respectively). The Parke County footprints measured twenty-one inches long. French Lick's ten-foot visitor (March 1965) earned the nickname "Fluorescent Freddie" for its glowing red eyes. A farmer near Delphi allegedly shot a five-foot-tall primate in May 1968. It escaped on all fours, and while blood was found at the scene, it was not preserved or tested. Parke County's hairy prowler reportedly killed two dogs.[8]

The decade's most peculiar Bigfoot sighting occurred at Rising Sun, in Ohio County, on May 19, 1969. The previous day, farmer Lester Keiser reported a loss of electric power, while his neighbors claimed sightings of unidentified flying objects (UFOs). Then, at 7:30 p.m. on May 19, George Keiser (Lester's son) saw a shaggy black biped "with no neck" standing in the barnyard. It was the size of an average human, some five feet seven inches tall. As Keiser approached, it made grunting sounds, then leapt over a ditch and fled, running upright. The Keisers made plaster casts of its strange four-toed footprints.[9]

The 1970s

The busy 1970s produced at least thirty-five alleged Bigfoot encounters from twenty-one Indiana counties, including six from Kosciusko County. Three sightings each emerged from Ohio and

Putnam Counties. Counties with two sightings each included Cass, Hamilton, Howard, Johnson, and Madison. Twenty-seven reports involved live sightings of large unknown primates, while eight were limited to footprints, odors, or unexplained vocalizations.[10]

Witnesses from this decade described bipedal creatures ranging from seven to twelve feet tall, sometimes exuding an odor like dead fish or sewage. Parke County's shaggy visitor of September 1972 may have been the same one seen six years earlier, since it left near-identical tracks twenty-one inches long. Witness Jerry Glass claimed that the creature he saw in Boone County (December 1977) "looked exactly like" the presumed Sasquatch filmed by Roger Patterson in California, ten years earlier. In two cases, witnesses at Galveston (October 1973) and Waterloo (September 1975) reported apelike creatures walking in proximity to UFOs. No dogs suffered from their encounters with the unknown primates, but Jackie Tharp of Williams (Lawrence County) claimed that a hairy creature grabbed her arm in December 1977. It fled when she screamed, leaving thirteen-inch tracks.[11]

In early August 1972, an unknown primate laid siege to the farm occupied by Randy and Lou Rogers outside Roachdale, in Putnam County. Growling noises from the woods came first, followed by neighbors' reports of airborne "luminous objects." Next, a foul-smelling prowler circled the farmhouse, slapping the walls and windows. Randy borrowed a gun and stood guard, reporting multiple sightings of a six-foot-tall hairy primate over the next three weeks. It walked upright but left no footprints, even in fresh mud. Sometimes it peered at Mrs. Rogers through the kitchen windows. When she put out leftovers to tempt the beast, it greedily consumed the food. The story went public on August 22, when some predator killed sixty chickens on Carter Burdine's nearby farm. Soon, fifty-odd locals claimed sightings of Bigfoot. Burdine fired on the beast when it returned to kill another 110 chickens, but it escaped, apparently unharmed.[12]

Tom and Connie Courter, of Rising Sun (Ohio County), played unwelcome hosts to a larger Bigfoot in April 1977. Their first sighting occurred at 11 p.m. on April 12, when the Courters returned to their mobile home from date. Out of the darkness, a twelve-foot-tall creature charged at their car and slammed into it, denting one side. Police investigated, but found no other trace of the prowler. The next night, at 11:45 p.m., the Courters heard "a real funny noise" from the woods, then saw Bigfoot perched atop a nearby hill. Tom fired fifteen shots from a .22-caliber rifle, driving the creature away for good. Again, police were summoned, but in vain.[13]

Hunters and hikers report Bigfoot encounters from Hoosier woodland settings. *Courtesy William Rebsamen.*

The 1980s

Hoosier witnesses reported thirty-four specific Bigfoot encounters from twenty counties in the 1980s. Nine counties boasted multiple sightings: three each from Knox, Lawrence, Martin, Monroe, and Perry; two each from Jackson, Kosciusko, La Porte, and Vermillion. Twenty-five reports involved live sightings, while nine were limited to sounds, odors, and similar evidence.[14]

Indiana primates described during the 1980s ranged from five to nine feet tall, variously sporting black, brown, and gray hair. One seen in Vanderburgh County had "oddly shaped" eye sockets, while a small specimen in Martin County was allegedly blind in one eye. Humanoid footprints discovered in Pulaski County, during winter 1988, measured fourteen inches long. Around the same time, in Vermillion County, witnesses supposedly recovered "unusual hair" from the woods where they watched a large primate voice "diabolical screams," but no scientific analysis followed. A Kosciusko County witness watched Bigfoot wade waist-deep in Yellow Creek Lake, apparently washing its face.[15]

Some of the most dramatic Bigfoot sightings are anonymous, like the story told to Gulf Coast Bigfoot Research Organization (GCBRO) investigators by a supposed witness in Martin County. According to that statement, the witness encountered at least three different primates during 1984-85. They ranged from five to six feet in height, with the smallest one blind in one eye. The mid-sized creature "had a mask" and shared food with the witness's dogs on his porch. The witness also claims that he (or she) "fed one that was crippled all winter," sending off hair samples and audio tapes of its voice to "a place" in Illinois, without result. In years past, the witness wrote, he lost livestock to predatory bipeds. Most astounding of all, the witness claimed that his uncle and grandfather captured a newborn primate after their hunting dogs cornered its mother. The female's fate is undisclosed, but the hunters allegedly gave the infant to a game warden, after which "all evidence of it disappeared [and] my grandfather's dogs were slaughtered." On balance, the tale sounds like fantasy, but without further identifying details we can say no more.[16]

Another curious tale emerged from southern Knox County in October 1981. After two sightings of a large unknown primate along the White River, Terry and Mary Harper reported that an unknown prowler had attacked their home on South 15th Street, in Vincennes. According to the Harpers, some unseen creature ripped and gnawed their aluminum siding, tearing off part of the backdoor's metal trim. It left bloodstains, teeth marks, and two-inch tufts of white hair at the scene, while inflicting some five hundred dollars in damage. Sheriff's deputies informed the Harpers that the blood was not human, but they attempted no further identification.[17]

The 1990s

Indiana produced eighteen specific Bigfoot reports in the final decade of the twentieth century. Eighteen of those reports spanned fourteen counties, while no location was provided for the nineteenth. Two counties—Harrison and Kosciusko—recorded multiple sightings, with two and three reports, respectively. Twelve of the reports included live sightings, while six involved humanoid tracks and/or unexplained noises.[18]

While most Hoosier reports from the 1990s simply describe "large" bipedal creatures, one Jefferson County witness pegged his specimen's height at five inches above his own six feet one. A Kosciusko witness reported a close encounter in his own yard, where a "very wet" Bigfoot approached and touched his arm, leaving his shirtsleeve damp when he fled to the nearby house. In November 1996, a mother and daughter in Floyd County saw an apelike creature sitting on a roadside log, near Edwardsville. The hulking jaywalker that startled a Bartholomew County motorist in winter 1992, west of Columbus, was "white and furry." The decade ended with a discovery of fresh three-toed tracks, some nine inches long and six inches across at their widest point, from a creek bed in Greene County's Centre Township.[19]

The decade's most dramatic report, once again collected by the GCBRO, describes the encounter claimed by two hunters—one called "Timmy," the other unnamed—at an undisclosed location in the Hoosier State. The GCBRO's failure to identify the county, if nothing more, remains unexplained. As detailed in the story, Timmy and friend were using a call "like a wounded rabbit" to attract small game, when they suddenly met a hairy biped eight or nine feet tall. Timmy fired a shotgun blast, then fled with his friend. The shrieking beast chased them for half a mile, then gave up. Returning the next day, the hunters found oversized humanoid footprints and spatters of blood on the foliage.[20]

Monsters for a New Millennium

At press time for this work, the twenty-first century had produced thirty-nine Bigfoot reports from twenty Indiana counties, plus six more whose locations were unspecified. Counties with multiple reports on file included Jennings (two), Kosciusko (eight), Monroe (three), Orange (two), and Perry (three). Twenty-three reports included live sightings, while sixteen involved only tracks, sounds, or odors.[21]

As in prior centuries, Hoosier witnesses offer various descriptions for the unknown primates seen since 2000. Most stand between seven and nine feet tall, while others are simply described as "way taller" than a six-foot witness or "easily twice the size" of a witness weighing 230 pounds. Hair color ranges from "orangish" to brown, gray, and black; where its length is described, it may be three to six inches long. At least five sightings involved multiple witnesses—and more surprisingly, two cases involved multiple creatures. A Vigo County fisherman sighted a Bigfoot "family" near Seeleyville, in October 2001, and witnesses in Kosciusko County saw two primates walking together near Waubee Lake, on April 2, 2004.[22]

At 3:30 p.m. on January 30, 2002, witnesses Penny Howell and Dale Moore saw an apelike creature crouching beside Chapel Hill Road, near the entrance to Monroe County's Hardin Ridge Recreation Area. They described the beast as five feet tall, weighing at least 200 pounds. It was covered with long dark hair, except for a white patch down the back of its head and neck. Its four-toed tracks, clearly impressed on damp clay, measured five inches long by four inches wide, with claw marks plainly visible on many of the footprints. Claw marks on one track measured 1.5 inches long, which ruled out a cougar as the culprit. Likewise, since the beast had only four toes, it could not have been a bear. As reported by journalist Kurt Van der Dussen, state officials and Indiana University anthropologist Dick Adams "aren't ruling out the possibility that [it]...could be some sort of ape." Adams opined that the witnesses might have glimpsed a sloth bear (*Melursus ursinus*) but he rightly judged a sighting of that Southeast Asian creature in the Hoosier State "pretty unlikely."[23]

Eleven months later, reporter Brian Hartz announced that the mystery was solved. His source for that conclusion was Dick Adams, who had since retired from Indiana University (in June 2002) after forty-seven years on the faculty. The creature's tracks, Adams now claimed, had "turned out to be nothing," while hairs recovered from the scene "were actually left by a large dog." According to Adams, "The whole thing is either a fraud or somebody had too much to drink." Expanding his judgment to include cougar reports, Adams said, "One time, they tried to make-believe there was a big cat or mountain lion in the area. Scientifically, there was nothing there. It's a matter of wanting something exciting. They want to believe that there's something different, exotic....We continue to hope that there's something different to find, but there never is."[24]

In fact, the solution offered by Adams—whom Hartz dubs "a veteran hoax-buster"—contains several obvious flaws.[25] Despite his confident, authoritative tone, important questions remain unanswered.

First, while anyone is free to offer an opinion on the subject, we may question why an anthropologist—one who devotes his life to study of human beings and their cultures—should be called to identify animal tracks. The DNR and Indiana University have trained zoologists on staff who are better qualified for that assignment. And why was Adams's final pronouncement delayed for nearly a year?

Next, it is erroneous to say that the Hardin Ridge tracks "turned out to be nothing." They were seen, described, measured—and perhaps photographed, though we cannot confirm it. Clearly, they were *something*. As to *what* they were or how they were created, Adams offers no suggestion, but they *did exist*. His statement of dismissal, as it stands, is meaningless.

Regarding hairs from Hardin Ridge—never mentioned in the original media reports—Adams offers no pertinent information. When, where, and by whom were they collected? Who claims that they came from the creature reported on January 30, 2002? Where, when, and by whom were they analyzed? Is a report of that analysis available? Why was the revelation sidetracked for eleven months? Without those answers, the convenient dog hypothesis remains suspect.

Adams's cougar diversion does not lend credence to his scientific objectivity. "They"—presumably the dozens of Hoosier witnesses spanning decades—*did not* "try to make-believe there was a big cat in the area." Rather, they reported events, including fatal attacks on domestic animals, which DNR agents acknowledge as factual, if still unexplained.

The professor's assertion that "[t]he whole thing is either a fraud or somebody had too much to drink" is both defamatory and fatally self-contradictory. No one suggests that witnesses Howell and Moore were drunk on the afternoon of January 30, 2002, and Adams dares not accuse them by name. At the same time, his drunk-and-delusional scenario cancels out any claim of a deliberate hoax—for which no evidence exists, in any case. It may be one or the other, not both, and Adams fails to prove his case for either.

Finally, we should note that while wishful thinking and "wanting something exciting" may influence eyewitness perceptions, perhaps causing a nervous hiker to mistake a bear for Bigfoot, a yen to believe in "something exotic" does not create footprints. It does not strip siding from homes and leave bloodstains or teeth marks. It does not kill livestock or dogs. Professor Adams fails in his attempt to do the opposite, using denial to make physical evidence vanish.

Desperately Seeking Sasquatch

Whatever Indiana's mystery primates may turn out to be, they have attracted a devoted group of followers. Those who go searching for the creature(s) may do well to concentrate in areas where Bigfoot leaves its tracks most often. Three such counties—Lawrence, Monroe, and Perry—lie within or adjacent to the sprawling Hoosier National

Forest, a protected wilderness area spanning some 400 square miles in south-central Indiana. To date, Lawrence and Perry boast eight specific sightings each, while Monroe claims six. Curiously, Indiana's greatest Bigfoot "hot spot" lies eighty-odd miles farther north, in Kosciusko County, with nineteen specific sightings on file.[26]

It is thus no surprise that that Indiana's premier "Bigfooter," Mike Bardsley, operates his Indiana Bigfoot Awareness Group from North Webster, in Kosciusko County. Bardsley's interest in cryptozoology dates from the predawn hours of October 10, 2003, when his son and two friends returned home from a high-school activity, describing in a "jumbled mess of excitement" their meeting with a hulking, hairy primate. Although initially incredulous, Bardsley listened to the tale and soon began to research other Bigfoot sightings in the Hoosier State and nationwide. Today, as he told journalist Scott Weisser in August 2005, Bardsley ranks himself as "a level three believer"—one who accepts the existence of Bigfoot without having seen the beast himself. He collects and publishes Hoosier sightings on an internet website, while suggesting that Bigfoot may be a migratory animal, wandering throughout North America at will.[27]

Mike Bardsley heads the Indiana Bigfoot Awareness Group. *Courtesy Stacey Staley and the Milford Mail-Journal.*

Bigfoot has been seen in these Kosciusko County woods. *Courtesy Stacey Staley and the Milford Mail-Journal.*

This Kosciusko County swamp has also produced Bigfoot sightings. *Courtesy Stacey Staley and the Milford Mail-Journal.*

What Are They?

Various authors advance diverse explanations for the global Big-foot/Yeti phenomenon. Those raised most often in regard to North America—and, by extension, to the Hoosier State—include:

(1) Hoaxes. No one disputes that certain Bigfoot sightings, photographs, and footprints have been faked over the past half-century or longer. Documented frauds include cases from California, Louisiana, Minnesota, Pennsylvania, and Virginia. Heated debate still surrounds the 1967 Patterson film and the "Minnesota Iceman," displayed at traveling carnivals during 1967-69. That said, it beggars belief that hoaxers are responsible for *all* sightings of Bigfoot and its tracks, reported nationwide since the early nineteenth century. Sightings and discovery of footprints in remote locations, miles off any beaten path, argue persuasively against legions of hoaxers dressed in ape suits, hobbling through woods and swamps on giant hand-carved feet. Likewise, dermal ridges found on certain footprint casts convince forensics experts that the feet which made the prints were flesh and blood, while other prints impressed in compact soil suggest a creature weighing upwards of 400 pounds. A standing reward of $100,000 for any hoaxer who can fool a panel of experts with fake Bigfoot tracks remains uncollected.[28]

(2) Bears. Whenever skeptics grant that Bigfoot witnesses may have seen *something*, they propose a case of mistaken identity, substituting some well-known species of wildlife for unknown primates. Bears fit the bill most closely, in terms of stature when standing erect, and they can also waddle upright when required to do so, for

Bears standing erect may be mistaken for Bigfoot—but they are officially extinct in Indiana. *Courtesy Tony Martin clipart © 2005.*

short distances. A Kodiak bear (*Ursus arctos middendorffi*) may rival Bigfoot's dimensions while standing upright, with a record length of 10.5 feet and a top weight of 900 pounds. Its rear feet may also measure sixteen inches long and ten inches wide—but the species lives only in Alaska. Farther south, grizzly bears may leave eleven-inch tracks, while skeptics suggest that overlapping prints from smaller brown or black bears may be mistaken for titanic humanoid tracks. That theory hits a snag with the presumed extinction of Indiana's only bear species (*U. americanus*) in 1850—although, as we have seen, sightings of black bears in the Hoosier State continue to the present day.[29]

(3) Known primates. If honest Bigfoot witnesses have not seen bears, skeptics insist, then they must have seen primates of some well-known species, either escaped from a circus or zoo, or released to the wild

African gorillas are Earth's largest known apes. *Courtesy PD Photo.org.*

by some negligent private owner. Since most Bigfoot reports describe creatures ranging from five to ten feet tall or larger, even with allowance for exaggeration by excited witnesses, the field of prospects is extremely limited. Three candidates, in order of descending size, include the gorilla (Genus *Gorilla,* with four subspecies recognized), the orangutan (Genus *Pongo,* two species), and the chimpanzee (*Pan troglodytes*). Male gorillas sometimes reach 6 feet in height, while male orangutans may reach 4.5 feet, and male chimpanzees reach full growth at 4 feet. (Females are smaller in all species.) Arguments against feral apes in the Hoosier State include their relatively small sizes, the fact that they rarely walk upright for any great distance, and the complete dissimilarity of their hand-shaped footprints from Bigfoot's humanoid tracks. Furthermore, no zoo or circus within living memory has reported a great ape's escape in Indiana.[30]

Asian orangutans are sometimes proposed as Bigfoot candidates, although none should be found in Indiana. *Courtesy PD Photo.org.*

African chimpanzees do not reach the size of creatures reported by most Bigfoot witnesses. *Courtesy FreeStockPhotos.com.*

(4) *Gigantopithecus blacki.* Many cryptozoologists have nominated this huge prehistoric ape as a Bigfoot/Yeti candidate worldwide, although it is known only from fossilized teeth and jaw fragments found in Asia. Based on those relics, dated between 125,000 and 500,000 years old by various researchers, "Giganto" stood nine to ten feet tall and tipped the scales between 650 and 1,200 pounds. If it had crossed the Bering Strait ice bridge to enter North America, and if it still survived today, the beast *might* be Bigfoot. Mainstream scientists dismiss any possibility of Giganto's survival, while noting that it is a distant relative of the orangutan, unlikely to possess humanoid feet. Some skeptics grant that ancient humans may have known Giganto in the flesh and passed on legends of the giant ape, which linger as aboriginal tales of forest-dwelling wildmen.[31]

(5) *Homo sapiens neanderthalensis.* Cryptozoologists Bernard Heuvelmans and Boris Porshnev, writing in 1974, proposed that Neandertal man—presumed extinct for 30,000 years—may still exist in some parts of the world, thus accounting for reports of certain unknown primates. At a record height of five feet seven inches, Neandertals could never match the larger primates seen by Bigfoot witnesses, but Heuvelmans and Porshnev thought they might explain the Minnesota Iceman, as well as certain hominids reported from Russia through Southeast Asia.[32]

(6) *Homo erectus.* Longtime Bigfoot researcher Ray Crowe suggests this predecessor of the Neandertals, presumed extinct for some 200,000 years, as an alternate candidate. Extinction aside, fossil remains indicate that *H. erectus* was slightly shorter than Neandertal man, on average, which argues against its candidacy in a majority of Bigfoot sightings.[33]

(7) *Homo heidelbergensis.* The direct ancestor of Neandertal man in Europe, *H. heidelbergensis* is named for a fossil jaw fragment found near Heidelberg, Germany, in 1906. That and other remains average 500,000 years in age, and the species is presumed extinct. Nonetheless, and despite its distinctly average human size, researcher Will Duncan proposes *H. heidelbergensis* as a rather unlikely Bigfoot candidate.[34]

(8) *Meganthropus.* Suggested as a possible North American primate by Loren Coleman, *Meganthropus* is known from a series of fossil jaw and skull fragments found on Java between 1933 and 1982. Two of the jaws, unearthed in 1945 and 1953, are roughly equal in size to the jaw of a modern gorilla. Others are smaller, prompting some paleoanthropologists to classify *Meganthropus* as a relative of *Homo erectus.* Whatever its final classification and overall size, no evidence presently exists that *Meganthropus* ever strayed outside present-day Indonesia.[35]

(9) Native primates. While North America presently harbors no recognized native primates except *Homo sapiens*—a species transplanted from Asia—other primates roamed the continent in prehistoric times. None were large, and paleontologists date their respective extinctions between 64 million years ago (*Purgatorius*) and 28 million years (*Ekgmowechashala*). Even if some, or all, of them survived to modern times, their size and physiology makes them unlikely Bigfoot candidates (though some might pass for Loren Coleman's "devil monkeys").[36]

What, then, is Bigfoot? How do we explain the great discrepancies in size and color, or the not-infrequent reports of anomalous three- and four-toed tracks? At present, we can only say that Indiana witnesses have seen *something* over the past 167 years that remains unexplained, but which is worthy of continued research.

Chapter 10
STRANGER YET

As strange as the encounters covered in the past nine chapters are, some still remain that manage to surpass them. None are classifiable within the other categories treated previously, so they stand collected here, a band of misfits offered for consideration at the reader's leisure. In the absence of a rational taxonomy, their stories are presented chronologically.

Wolfmen (18th Century)

French trappers blazed the Hoosier State's first trails, and they brought with them legends of the *loup-garous* ("wolf-men"), best known to modern-day Americans from their depiction in assorted horror films. Wherever Frenchmen traveled in those early days, the *loup-garou* followed, and if their stories are believed, it was a hungry thing of flesh and blood.[1]

Knox County historians have done the best job of preserving wolfman tales in Indiana, but the creatures they describe were not always human beings who changed into wolves. In fact, some willingly transformed themselves into cattle, horses, and other animals, though they were uniformly vicious when in beastly form. Nor were they bound by any cycles of the moon. Instead, French storytellers claimed, the *loup-garou* might lose himself in the form of some alternate species for up to 101 days at a time, during which it was fatal for any mere human to meet him (or her) in the wild.[2]

Strangely, despite that malevolent mien, some of Indiana's more famous shape-shifters proved to be benevolent for certain human friends. The White Eagle *loup-garou* befriended a hunter named

Soudeniere and nursed him through critical illness. At Vincennes, a "good pumpkin *loup-garou*" rescued pumpkin-loving farmer Jacques Cabaisser after his horse plunged into an icy river. A "cow *loup-garou*" intervened to help American forces defeat British soldiers, during the Revolutionary War. A "horse *loup-garou*" named Jean Baptiste allegedly learned how to fly.[3]

It is easy to dismiss such tales as fantasy. However, "werewolf" sightings have continued to the present day in Wisconsin, Illinois, and elsewhere, as detailed by author Linda Godfrey in her best-selling books *The Beast of Bray Road* (2003) and *Hunting the American Werewolf* (2006). In light of those reports, outright dismissal may be ill-advised.

Werewolves feature in many early Indiana legends—and some modern-day sightings from neighboring states. *Courtesy William Rebsamen.*

Tippecanoe River Monsters (1871)

Despite its title, bestowed by Fulton County historian Shirley Willard in 2000, the Tippecanoe River Monster was neither an aquatic creature nor a solitary specimen. In fact, its description—offered to Marshall County's *Bourbon Mirror* by correspondent "A. K. B." in January 1872—was very different indeed.

According to A. K. B.'s letter, published on January 14: "For some months past this vicinity has been infested with two of the most uncouth looking animals that were ever seen, and so piercing were their hideous screams that it shook everybody with awe that heard them." The beasts roamed freely along the Tippecanoe River, from Atwood to Bloomingsburg, but appeared most often in or near Devil Swamp, south of Tiptown. They terrorized local farmers, slaughtering calves, hogs, and sheep, while eluding the few hunters who dared to pursue them.[4]

At last, on December 21, 1871, intrepid locals J. H. Debolt and Del Latham set out with "plenty of arms" and a half-dozen dogs to destroy the creatures. After a rigorous two-mile pursuit, they met the beasts in a thicket, where a fight to the death ensued. The hunters wounded both animals with rifle shots, then closed with knives. Despite help from their dogs, both men were badly wounded in the melee. Latham suffered a fractured skull when his rifle exploded, regaining consciousness to find Debolt with one arm nearly severed. Snatching up Debolt's rifle, Latham finished one of the beasts with a shot to the head, while its mate escaped. Debolt subsequently lost his arm, but Dr. Milton Hall predicted that both hunters would survive their wounds.[5]

Back at the battle scene, friends of the injured men "found the ground strewed with blood, bloody knives, broken firearms, pieces of wearing apparel and dead dogs, all presenting scenes of a bloody struggle. The animal killed was found, by measurement[,] to be six feet and nine inches in length and two feet and nine inches in height, and weighed two hundred and seventeen pounds. Its hide was taken and can be seen at the store in Bloomingsburg. The teeth and feet are on exhibition at the office of Dr. Hall, in Tiptown."[6]

Sadly, while the communities remain—Tiptown, with thirty-odd inhabitants in 1990, qualified for "ghost town" status—no further record of the local monsters now survives. The slaughtered beast's remains have long since vanished. Shirley Willard, in 2000, asked "Was this like the fabled Bigfoot?" but the contemporary description hardly resembles the familiar apelike creature standing six to eight feet tall. Instead, it almost sounds catlike, though A. K. B. avoided comparison to any known species.[7] The mystery remains unsolved.

Jacob Rishel's Dragon (1879)

Our next tale comes from the *Fort Wayne Sentinel,* published on August 20, 1879. According to that story, farmer Jacob Rishel was passing through a field in Jackson Township, northeast of town, on August 16, when he "noticed the tall grass waving about and being agitated in a very violent manner, having the exact appearance of a small whirlwind." Turning to flee, Rishel was further frightened when the "wind" changed course to follow him. Moments later, the grass parted to reveal "a huge reptile or monster the like of which he had never seen before."[8]

Rishel ran for his life, but the monster kept pace, drawing so close that Rishel later claimed, "I could smell his breath." It seemed to be a huge snake, but with horns or tentacles protruding from its head above each eye. After a harrowing pursuit, Rishel reached a fence where a convenient scythe hung waiting, and he snatched the weapon, turning to confront the beast. His first blow severed one of its "horns," and Rishel finally managed to kill the reptile, cutting off its head after the monster snagged its body on the prongs of a reaping machine.[9]

Securing assistance from a group of unnamed friends, Rishel proceeded to assess his kill. According to the *Sentinel*, "the snake was laid out and found by actual measurement to be 34 feet and 3 inches in length and about as thick as a barrel....The tentacles spoken of were about forty-two inches long and about three inches in diameter where they joined the head. The head was remarkably small for the size of the snake and was flat, something of the nature of a flat-head snake. The color was precisely like that of the garter snake on a larger scale with a dark green stripe running down its back. The snake was skinned and the skin sent to Chicago where it will be stuffed and placed on exhibition."[10]

It goes without saying that no such trophy reached the Windy City, and no record of its shipment now remains. Since neither Rishel nor the *Sentinel* presumed to state where they had sent the skin, the trail ends there, in mystery.

Sightings of huge serpents or dragons are common to all human cultures. *Courtesy Tony Martin clipart © 2005.*

Flying Fish (1888)

Our next story appeared in the *Newark* (Ohio) *Daily Advance* on August 4, 1888, reporting an event from Seymour, Indiana, three days earlier. That brief snippet read: "During a heavy storm Wednesday night a large number of fish, of a variety unknown here, some of them four inches in length, fell in this neighborhood. The occurrence excited a good deal of curiosity, but no one has been able to explain the phenomenon."[11]

And so it remains today, although odd "rains"—including flesh and blood, live animals, and stones—have been recorded throughout human history. Such eerie falls continue to the present day, poorly explained by mainstream scientists (when they attempt explanations at all).[12]

A Flying Monster (1891)

Tireless researcher Charles Fort uncovered our next strange report, buried in the pages of the *Brooklyn* (N.Y.) *Eagle* on September 10, 1891. According to that report, two icemen in Crawfordsville, Indiana, beheld a "seemingly headless monster" soaring overhead in the early hours of September 5. It was some twenty feet long and eight feet wide, propelled by flapping wings. Its noisy flight woke a Methodist clergyman, Rev. G. W. Switzer, who watched it from his bedroom window.[13]

Ever skeptical, Fort presumed the story to be false and Switzer nonexistent, until further research confirmed a Rev. Switzer's presence in Crawfordsville during September 1891. Fort traced Switzer to Michigan and wrote to him there. Switzer replied that he was embarking on a trip to California, but promised a full description of the creature upon his return. Sadly, Switzer did not write again before Fort published the story in 1931.[14]

"Mud Mermaids" (1894)

In autumn 1894, the *Cincinnati Enquirer* published an anonymous letter, reprinted in the *Sandusky Register* on October 19, which described a curious event at Vevay, Indiana, on the Ohio River in Switzerland County. According to that report, "two nondescript creatures horrible in appearance and habit" had displayed themselves on an offshore sand bank. While dubbing them "mud mermaids," the nameless correspondent wrote: "They are amphibious in nature and resemble in appearance huge lizards with human features." They allegedly subsisted on a diet of fish, mussels, and other aquatic prey.[15]

According to the letter, sightings of the "mermaids"—who appeared to be a mated pair—had begun in 1891, climaxed in 1894 when Kentucky artist "Captain J. M. Ozier" observed the male specimen and prepared several sketches (not included with the letter).[16] According to Ozier:

> The body between the fore legs resembles that of a human being. Back of the hind legs it tapers to a point. This point in no way resembles a tail. The legs, four in number, resemble the arms and legs of the human. The fore legs are shorter than the hind pair and are used in the same manner as arms. The extremities resemble hands and are webbed and furnished with claws. On the back and one-third of the way around the body appears a mass of straggling, coarse hair. The skin below the fore legs is thick and resembles elephant hide. On the

arms and about the face and neck it is of a finer texture and brighter yellow color than the rest of the body."[17]

The creature's face was "strikingly human," but sported doglike ears and "bore no signs of intelligence." Ozier further opined that the beast "resembles to a great extent the freak known as Zip, or the What-is-It, which was exhibited first by P. T. Barnum."[18] Whether that addendum proves a hoax or not, I leave to the discretion of my readers.

Witnesses reported two "mud mermaids" from Vevay, Indiana, in 1894. *Courtesy Tony Martin clipart © 2005.*

The Pukwudgee (1927)

Native American legends are rife with tales of forest-dwelling "little people," known by various names among different tribes. Midwestern Delaware and Wampanoag tribesmen knew them as *Pukwasjiineesuk* ("little Indians"), *Pukwatcininins* ("little man of the woods"), or *Pukwud-jie,* Anglicized to the modern term "Pukwudgee." According to legend, they averaged two feet in height, had light skin and light brown hair. The Pukwudgee wore shirts made of grass or bark, and built small houses out of sticks and grass. Most aborigines considered them human, rather than creatures of spirit.[19]

In June 1927, while hiking along Indiana's White River, ten-year-old Paul Startzman found an abandoned gravel pit and there met a two-foot-tall man wearing a light blue robe. "We stood about ten yards apart and looked at each other," Startzman later said. "He had thick, dark blond hair, and his face was round and pinkish in color, like it was sunburned." After a moment, the tiny barefoot figure turned and fled into the woods.[20]

A short time later, Startzman met a similar little man in the same vicinity, this time while hiking with a friend. Instead of fleeing at once, the Pukwudgee followed Startzman and his companion for a while, before melting into the forest. Startzman subsequently told his story to television reporters. It may (or may not) be significant that his mother was a full-blooded Amerindian.[21]

Big Bird (1946)

As little people flourish in aboriginal legends, so do mighty "thunderbirds," described as massive super-eagles capable of hunting man-sized prey. Sightings of birds surpassing any modern species in sheer size continue to the present day, across America, but Indiana's sole report on file (so far) dates from the postwar year of 1946.

The tale properly begins in April 1948, when numerous reports of a huge bird at large were filed by witnesses in Illinois and Missouri. After two St. Louis policemen and a local chiropractor saw the bird, Mayor Aloys Kaufmann demanded action. His aide, Charles Hertenstein, promptly produced reports suggesting that the bird was a great blue heron (*Ardea herodias*), whose wingspan may reach six feet.[22]

That explanation failed to wash with local witnesses, but more importantly, it prompted a resident of Bowling Green, Indiana, to write Hertenstein about his own experience from 1946. According to that unnamed witness, he had seen a bird "the size of a twelve-hundred pound horse."[23]

Almost incredibly, there *were* such giant birds in days gone by. The largest flying (as opposed to flightless) bird now known to science was *Argentavis magnificens,* a vulture of Late Miocene Argentina, presumed extinct for some five million years. *Argentavis* stood five to six feet tall at rest and weighed 158 pounds, boasting a twenty-five-foot wingspan. Two smaller relatives from North America, *Teratornis incrediblis* and *T. merriami,* boasted wingspreads of nineteen and twelve feet, respectively. Meanwhile, the largest known flying creature of all time was *Quetzalcoatlus,* a reptile from Late Cretaceous North

America, with a wingspan of thirty-nine feet.[24] Mainstream science, naturally, rejects the notion that any such creatures still visit American skies.

The teratorn, presumed extinct today, was large enough to qualify as a mythical "thunderbird." *Courtesy FreeStockPhotos.com.*

The Dogtown "Lizard Man" (1955)

Our final entry in the great what-was-it contest was *felt,* rather than seen, on August 21, 1955. That muggy afternoon, Mrs. Darwin Johnson and a friend, Mrs. Chris Lamble, went swimming in the Ohio River near Dogtown, a few miles upriver from Evansville, in Vanderburgh County. While clinging to an inner tube, some fifteen feet offshore, Johnson felt something like a hand grasp her left leg at the knee, pulling her underwater. She kicked free, but the unseen grappler seized her again and once more yanked her head beneath the surface. Again, she fought her way to fresh air, but the creature—if creature it was—retained a firm grip. Only when Lamble swam to help her friend, both women screaming, did the clutching hand withdraw.[25]

Mrs. Johnson said the hand that grabbed her had clawed fingers and a "furry" palm. Fortean investigator Terry Colvin subsequently reported that Johnson's left leg bore a green stain, shaped like a palm print, "that could not be removed for several days." After the *Evansville Press* ran a short piece on the incident, several other locals claimed sightings of a "shiny oval" hovering over the river around the same time on August 21. Those UFO sightings, in turn, brought a United States Air Force officer to visit Johnson and her husband, grilling them about the incident and taking detailed notes.[26]

Authors Jerome Clark and Loren Coleman published their first account of the Dogtown incident in 1978, as briefly summarized here. Four years later, repeating the tale in another book, Coleman alone suggested that the "furry" palm might have been "scaly," instead. He offered no reason for the change—fur and scales have little in common, by sight or by touch—but it stuck. In 2002, author George Eberhart listed Mrs. Johnson's encounter with six other North American "lizard man" sightings, spanning the continent from British Columbia to South Carolina in the years 1955-1988.[27]

Loren Coleman describes Dogtown's aquatic cryptid of 1955 as a "lizard man." *Courtesy William Rebsamen.*

Endnotes

Introduction
1. Coleman and Clark, pp. 15, 75.
2. Greenwell, p. 4.
3. Heuvelmans, p. 1.

Chapter 1
1. Simon et al., pp. 182, 192, 196-199, 214.
2. Ibid., pp. 194, 196, 199.
3. Ibid., p. 194.
4. Conant and Collins, pp. 537-538.
5. Ibid., pp. 532-533; Simon et al., p. 194.
6. Conant and Collins, pp. 548-549.
7. Ibid., pp. 551-552.
8. Ibid., pp. 481-483.
9. Ibid., pp. 484-485.
10. Simon et al., p. 196.
11. Conant and Collins, pp. 268-269.
12. Ibid., pp. 301-303.
13. Ibid., pp. 323-324.
14. Simon et al., p. 199.
15. North American Mammals.
16. Ibid.
17. Simon et al., pp. 192, 196, 199, 214; Allison, "Many species native to Indiana now face extinction."
18. Allison, op cit.; Conant and Collins, pp. 148, 335-336, 401-403; Simon et al., pp. 194, 196.
19. *Field Guide to the Birds of North America,* pp. 130, 138, 150, 166, 368; Simon et al., p. 214.

20. *Field Guide to the Birds of North America,* p. 284; Newton, pp. 88, 212-213; Shuker, "Alien zoo;" Simon et al., p. 214.
21. Allison, op cit.; Simon et al., pp. 200, 203, 205, 208.
22. Simon et al., p. 199.
23. North American Mammals; Simon et al., p. 199.
24. Allison, "Many species native to Indiana now face extinction;" Allison, "Sightings of large cats, bears reported," Allison, "Sometimes wild animals come back;" Slabaugh.
25. Allison, "Exotic species become state residents;" Simon et al., pp. 185-190, 200, 202, 203, 206, 210, 213, 214.
26. Simon et al., pp. 185-190, 192.
27. Catalog of the Species of Fishes; Allison, "Unusual species found on land, in water;" "Fisherman catches one piranha, others spotted in Indiana lake;" Seng and White.
28. Catalog of the Species of Fishes; Seng and White; Swaby.
29. Allison, "Unusual species found on land, in water;" Catalog of the Species of Fishes; Seng and White.
30. Allison, op cit.; Catalog of the Species of Fishes.
31. Seng and White.
32. Allison, "Exotic species become state residents;" *Field Guide to the Birds of North America,* pp. 66, 132, 234, 236, 358, 448, 456; Simon et al., pp. 202, 203, 206, 210, 213, 214.
33. Gillihan; Newton, p. 149.
34. Bridge; Mammal Species of the World; Simon et al., p. 198.
35. "Bowhunter bags British deer—in Indiana;" Mammal Species of the World; Simon et al., p. 199.
36. "Strange animal 'ferocious as a tiger' baffles community."
37. Mammal Species of the World; Newton, p. 152.
38. Arment and LaGrange, "The Crawford critter;" Mammal Species of the World; Simon et al., p. 198.

Chapter 2

1. Simon et al., pp. 194-196.
2. Ibid., pp. 195-196.
3. Day and Ingram.

4. "Latest snake story."
5. Conant and Collins, pp. 404-405; 408-409; Simon et al., p. 196.
6. Eberhart, p. 200.
7. "'He looked like a big white tree limb';" Freund; Koryta.
8. "Indiana's big snake."
9. Conant and Collins, pp. 233, 250, 262-263, 268, 276-278; Simon et al., pp. 195-196.
10. Halliday and Adler, p. 111; "Lizard eludes would-be captors in Brown County;" Van der Dussen, "Monitor lizard spotted near lake."
11. Leonard.
12. Conant and Collins, pp. 142-145; Halliday and Adler, p. 136.
13. Day.
14. Quoted in Bord and Bord, *Unexplained Mysteries,* p. 220.
15. LaGrange, "Cryptoherps;" "Petersburg lays claim to 'gator killed down-state."
16. LaGrange, op cit.
17. "Alligator found in Fall Creek;" Coleman, *Mysterious America,* p. 302; Spangle.
18. "Alligator found in retention pond likely abandoned pet;" "Alligator found in South Bend river is killed," "Alligator pulled from West Lafayette retention pond;" "Alligator spotted in South Bend river;" Gallegos; Johnson; Kunz; Levco; Seng and White.

Chapter 3

1. Conant and Collins, p. 148; Simon et al., pp. 194-195.
2. Repine; The Turtle in Missouri Folklore.
3. Gutowski, pp. 27-28.
4. Ibid., pp. 28-29, 131.
5. Ibid., pp. 30-32.
6. Ibid., pp. 32-33.
7. Ibid., pp. 34-35.
8. Ibid., pp. 36-39.
9. Ibid., p. 39.
10. Ibid., pp. 39-41.
11. Coleman and Huyghe, pp. 175-176; "Giant turtle?"; Gutowski, p. 42.

12. Gutowski, p. 57.
13. Ibid., pp. 57-58.
14. Ibid., p. 58.
15. Ibid., pp. 58-59.
16. Ibid., pp. 4, 84-103.
17. "Agency: Turtle not an animal;" "Judge rejects man's request to take turtles on tour;" "Man taking snapping turtle on tour;" The Turtle in Missouri Folklore.
18. "Beast of Busco."

Chapter 4

1. North American Mammals; Simon et al., p. 199.
2. Allison, "Sightings of large cats, bears reported;" Eastern Puma Research Network.
3. "Woman says what she saw looked like mountain lion."
4. "Cat suspected in car mauling."
5. McLaren.
6. "Photo fuels false cougar rumors."
7. Allison, op cit.
8. Ayi; "Here, kitty, kitty;" Kosky and Holmes.
9. "Officials do not confirm reported cougar sighting."
10. "Some say there is a cougar near town;" Van der Dussen, "Big cat? Big dog?"; Van der Dussen, "Is a cougar on the prowl near Griffy?"; Van der Dussen, "Speculation continues on cougar near Griffy;" Van der Dussen, "Woman spots 'huge cat'."
11. Van der Dussen, "Big cat? Big dog?"; Van der Dussen, "Woman trying to prove mystery critter's a cougar."
12. Van der Dussen, "Crane officer reports he saw a big cat."
13. Perrin.
14. Freitag; Van der Dussen, "Two more large cat sightings in Monroe."
15. "Mountain lion seized at home;" "Mountain lion shot, killed after escaping from car after crash."
16. Allison, "Sightings of large cats, bears reported;" Eastern Puma Research Network; Eberhart, p. 157; Leiser.

Chapter 5

1. Shuker, *Mystery Cats of the World.* pp. 24-26.
2. Coleman, *Mysterious America,* pp. 124-125.
3. Day.
4. Clark and Coleman, *Creatures of the Outer Edge,* p. 129.
5. Ibid., p. 130.
6. Ibid.
7. Ibid., pp. 130-131.
8. Ibid., p. 131.
9. Ibid., pp. 131-132; Coleman, *Mysterious America,* p. 130.
10. Clark and Coleman, op cit., p. 132.
11. Ibid., p. 133.
12. Ibid., pp. 132-133.
13. Ibid., p. 133.
14. Ibid., pp. 133-134.
15. Ibid., p. 134.
16. Ibid.
17. Shuker, *Mystery Cats,* pp. 28-30, 101-107, 132-133, 162.
18. Eastern Puma Research Network.
19. Clark and Coleman, op cit., p. 134; Coleman, *Mothman,* p. 156; Coleman, *Mysterious America,* p. 109; Glassing; LaGrange, "Black panther sighting;" LaGrange, "Black panthers in Perry County;" Van der Dussen, "Newspaper carrier reports black panther;" Van der Dussen, "Two more large cat sightings in Monroe."
20. Coleman and Clark, *Creatures of the Outer Edge,* p. 137-138; Coleman, *Mysterious America,* pp. 131, 155.
21. Bord and Bord, Unexplained Mysteries, p. 365.
22. Wilson.
23. Borelli.
24. McLaren.
25. Allison, "Sightings of large cats, bears reported;" Van der Dussen, "Woman sees cougar like animal along Tapp Road."
26. Perrin.

27. "Big cat blamed for killing pigs near Bloomington;" "Big panther-like cat blamed for killing pigs in Owen County, Ind.;" "Owen County couple say they saw panther."
28. Van der Dussen, "Animal mauls several dogs on northwest side;" Van der Dussen, "Couple''s dogs mauled."
29. Arment, "Black panthers in North America;" Shuker, *Mystery Cats,* p. 162.
30. Lutz, pp. 35-36.
31. Coleman, *Mysterious America,* pp. 150-159.

Chapter 6
1. Eberhart, p. 655.
2. Garner, p. 180.
3. Hess, pp. 3-5.
4. Ibid., pp. 5-6; "The Monster at Manitou."
5. Hess, p. 6; Smalley, p. 255.
6. Garner, p. 76; "The Monster at Manitou."
7. Marvin Allen, personal communication (30 May 2006); Hess, pp. 6-7.
8. "The devil caught at last;" Hess, p. 7.
9. List of Common Fish Names' Shirley Willard, personal communication (3 May 2006).
10. Carol Utter Johnson, personal communication (3 May 2006).
11. Shirley Willard, personal communication (3 May 2006).
12. Carol Young, personal communication (16 May 2006).
13. Hess, p. 7; Jeff Kenney, personal communication (3 May 2006).
14. Kenney, op cit.
15. Marvin Allen, personal correspondence (30 May 2006).
16. "Monsters of the deep."
17. Ibid.; Marvin Allen, personal correspondence (30 May 2006).
18. Day.
19. "A sea serpent."
20. Ibid.
21. Day; "A sea serpent."
22. Coleman, *Mysterious America,* p. 81; Day; "Sea serpent seen again."
23. Garner, p. 181; "Monsters of the Deep;" Skinner, Vol. 2, p. 298.
24. Shirley Willard, personal communication (3 May 2006).

25. Jones.

26. Ibid.

27. Coleman, *Mysterious America,* pp. 88-89; Coleman and Huyghe, p. 258; Garner, p. 181.

28. Ron Hamilton, personal communication (29 April 2006).

29. Ibid.

30. Ibid.

31. Ibid.

32. Eberhart, p. 682; "'Monster' or calf?"

33. Coleman, *Mysterious America,* p. 309; Kirk, p. 296; Newton, pp. 140-141; Online Lake Cryptid Directory.

Chapter 7

1. Burnie, p. 543.

2. Ibid.

3. Arment and LaGrange, "A freshwater octopus?", pp. 48-49.

4. Ibid., p. 49.

5. Ibid., pp. 47-48; Eberhart, p. 181.

6. Arment and LaGrange, op cit., pp. 50-51.

7. Swartz.

8. Bastide.

9. Bastide; Swartz.

10. Bastide.

11. Ibid.

12. Ibid.

Chapter 8

1. Newton, pp. 223-224, 480-481.

2. Coleman, *Mysterious America,* p. 172.

3. Ibid., p. 173.

4. Ibid.

5. "Animal Control investigates kangaroo sighting;" "Another roo on the loose;" Gallegos, "Blimey, mate."

6. "Animal Control investigates kangaroo sighting;" "Another roo on the loose;" Gallegos, "Blimey, mate."

7. Gallegos, "S.B. search called off for reported kangaroo."
8. Coleman, op cit., pp. 161-162, 184-187.
9. Ibid., p. 217; Eberhart, pp. 127-128.
10. Coleman, op cit., pp. 206-220; Newton, pp. 338-340.
11. Eberhart, pp. 390, 392.

Chapter 9

1. Bigfoot Field Researchers Organizations (hereafter BFRO); Bord and Bord, *Bigfoot Casebook,* pp. 151-230; Green, pp. 204-208; Gulf Coast Bigfoot Research Organization (hereafter GCBRO).
2. "A wild child."
3. "Beast or human being?"
4. "Resembles a man."
5. Green, p. 204.
6. BFRO Report No. 9245.
7. BFRO; GCBRO; Keel, p. 113.
8. Bord and Bord, op cit., pp. 67, 167, 169, 172; BFRO Reports No. 2462, 6534, 9245; GCRBO; Green, pp. 204-205.
9. Bord and Bord, op cit., p. 179; Green, p. 205; Keel, pp. 99-100.
10. BFRO; Bord and Bord, op cit., pp. 186, 188, 191, 192, 205, 220; GCBRO; Indiana Bigfoot Awareness Group (hereafter IBAG); Green, pp. 205-208; Rife, pp. 83-84.
11. BFRO Reports No. 2459, 6094, 10153, 10538; Bord and Bord, op cit., pp. 112-114, 186, 188, 191, 192, 205, 215, 220; GCBRO; Green, p. 206; Wibert.
12. Bord and Bord, op cit., pp. 109-110, 199; Clark and Coleman, *The Unidentified,* pp. 14-19.
13. Bord and Bord, op cit., p. 213; Clark and Coleman, op cit., p. 209; Green, p. 208.
14. BFRO; GCBRO; IABG.
15. BFRO Reports No. 2076, 2472, 2473, 3233, 7239; GCBRO; IBAG.
16. GCBRO.
17. BFRO Report No. 202; Carroll.
18. BFRO; GCBRO; IBAG.
19. BFRO Reports No. 292, 1696, 2457, 2467, 10678; GCBRO; IABG.

20. GCBRO.

21. BFRO; GCBRO; IABG.

22. BFRO Reports No. 3186, 3195, 4466, 8438, 9642, 13242; GCBRO; IABG Reports No. 0002-2004, 0008-2005, 0002-2006, 0003-2006.

23. Van der Dussen, "Anthropologist doubts creature is a sloth bear;" Van der Dussen, "Ape? Bear? Bigfoot?"

24. Hartz, "Case of the Bigfoot sighting solved."

25. Hartz, "Professor finds Bigfoot signs way off track."

26. BFRO; GCBRO; IABG.

27. IABG website; Weisser.

28. Newton, pp. 61-62, 196-197, 297-299.

29. Mammal Species of the World; Simon et al., p. 199.

30. Mammal Species of the World.

31. Newton, pp. 171-172.

32. Eberhart, pp. 13, 267, 339 , 387.

33. Ibid., p. 56.

34. Ibid.

35. Ibid.; "Meganthropus."

36. Eberhart, loc cit.

Chapter 10

1. Knox County Folklore, Legends and Tall Tales.

2. Ibid.

3. Ibid.

4. A.B.K.. "Tippecanoe correspondence."

5. Ibid.

6. Ibid.

7. Willard.

8. "A tale of terror."

9. Ibid.

10. Ibid.

11. "Fish from the clouds."

12. Clark, pp. xxviii-xxix.

13. Fort, p. 637.

14. Ibid., pp. 637-638.

15. "Mud mermaids."
16. Ibid.
17. Ibid.
18. Ibid.
19. Eberhart, p. 444.
20. Clark, p. 99; Eberhart, op cit.
21. Clark, op cit.; Eberhart, op cit.
22. Coleman, *Mothman,* pp. 69-70; *Field Guide to the Birds of North America,* p. 62.
23. Coleman, op cit., pp. 70-71.
24. Newton, pp. 456-457.
25. Clark and Coleman, *Creatures of the Outer Edge,* pp. 52-53; Coleman, op cit., pp. 93-94.
26. Clark and Coleman, loc cit.; Coleman, loc cit.
27. Clark and Coleman, loc cit.; Coleman, loc cit.; Eberhart, p. 298.

Sources

"About Monsters and Such." Vincennes (Ind.) *Valley Advance* (6 October 1981).

"Agency: Turtle not an animal." Bloomington (Ind.) *Herald-Times* (11 July 2002).

A. K. B., "Tippecanoe correspondence." *Bourbon* (Ind.) *Mirror* (19 January 1872).

"Alligator found in Fall Creek." Bloomington (Ind.) *Herald-Times* (27 August 1999).

"Alligator pulled from West Lafayette retention pond." Bloomington (Ind.) *Herald-Times* (27 July 2004).

"Alligator found in retention pond likely abandoned pet." Bloomington (Ind.) *Herald-Times* (11 August 2004).

"Alligator found in South Bend river is killed." Bloomington (Ind.) *Herald-Times* (8 June 2005).

"Alligator spotted in South Bend river." Munster (Ind.) *Times* (3 June 2005).

Allison, Harold. "Alien invaders take to the waters." Bloomington (Ind.) *Herald-Times* (3 April 2005).

_____. "Exotic species become state residents." Bloomington (Ind.) *Herald-Times* (20 March 2005).

_____. "Exotic species include the house finch." Bloomington (Ind.) *Herald-Times* (14 August 2005).

_____. "Exotic species take hold in Indiana, elsewhere." Bloomington (Ind.) *Herald-Times* (27 November 2005).

_____. "Hoosier rivers are still home to variety of fish." Bloomington (Ind.) *Herald-Times* (12 February 2006).

_____. "Many species native to Indiana now face extinction." Bloomington (Ind.) *Herald-Times* (12 August 2001).

_____. "Sightings of large cats, bears reported." Bloomington (Ind.) *Herald-Times* (2 May 2004).

_____. "Sometimes wild animals come back." Bloomington (Ind.) *Herald-Times* (2 November 2003).

_____. "Unusual species found on land, in water." Bloomington (Ind.) *Herald-Times* (21 October 2001).

Arment, Chad. "Black panthers in North America." *North American Bio-Fortean Review* 3 (2000): 38-56.

Arment, Chad, and Brad LaGrange. "The Crawford Critter or 'King Squirrel.'" *North American BioFortean Review* 5 (December 2000): 20.

_____ and _____. "A freshwater octopus?" *North American BioFortean Review* 5 (December 2000): 47-51.

Ayi, Mema. "Police using helicopter to track cougar." Munster (Ind.) *Times* (5 November 2004).

Bastide, Ken de la. "Creature in Plant 9 pits." *Anderson* (IN) *Herald Bulletin* (5 March 1997).

"Beast of Busco." Wikipedia, en.wikipedia.org/wiki/Beast_of_Busco.

"Beast or human being?" *Atchison* (Kan.) *Globe* (19 July 1883).

"Big cat blamed for killing pigs near Bloomington." *Indianapolis Star* (9 February 2006).

"Big cat sightings unconfirmed." *South Bend* (Ind.) *Tribune* (5 June 2006).

"Big panther-like cat blamed for killing pigs in Owen County, Ind." *South Bend* (Ind.) *Tribune* (10 February 2006).

Bigfoot Field Researchers Organization, www.bfro.net.

Bord, Janet, and Colin Bord. *The Bigfoot Casebook*. London Granada, 1982.

_____. *Bigfoot Casebook Updated*. Ravensdale, Wash.: Pine Winds Press, 2006.

_____. *Unexplained Mysteries of the 20th Century*. Chicago: Contemporary Books, 1989.

Borelli, Robert. "Possible panther sighting in South Bend." WNDU-TV, Channel 16 (6 October 2003).

"Bowhunter bags British deer—in Indiana." *Indianapolis Star* (6 October 2004).

Bridge, Bob. "Hunters bag two Russian boars." Bloomington (Ind.) *Herald-Times* (21 January 2001).

Burnie, David, ed. *Animal*. London: Dorling Kindersley, 2001.

Carroll, Doug. "Area Residents See 'Something Big and Hairy.'" Vincennes (Ind.) *Valley Advance* (6 October 1981).

"Cat suspected in car mauling." Bloomington (Ind.) *Herald-Times* (9 May 2003).

A Catalog of the Species of Fishes, www.calacademy.org/research/ichthyology/species.

Clark, Jerome. *Unnatural Phenomena*. Santa Barbara, Calif.: ABC-CLIO, 2005.

Clark, Jerome, and Loren Coleman. *Creatures of the Outer Edge*. New York: Warner Books, 1978.

_____ and _____. *The Unidentified*. New York: Warner Books, 1975.

Coghlan, Ronan. *A Dictionary of Cryptozoology*. Bangor: Xiphos Books, 2004.

Coleman, Loren. *Bigfoot!* New York: Paraview Pocket Books, 2003.

_____. *Mothman and Other Curious Encounters*. New York: Paraview Press, 2002.

_____. *Mysterious America*. New York: Paraview Press, 2001.

Coleman, Loren, and Jerome Clark. *Cryptozoology A to Z*. New York: Fireside, 1999.

Coleman, Loren, and Patrick Huyghe. *The Field Guide to Lake Monsters, Sea Serpents, and Other Mystery Denizens of the Deep*. New York: Tarcher/Penguin, 2003.

Conant, Roger, and Joseph Collins. *A Field Guide to Reptiles and Amphibians: Eastern and Central North America*, 3d ed. Boston: Houghton Mifflin, 1998.

"Cougar sightings hardly ridiculous." Bloomington (Ind.) *Herald-Times* (19 May 2005).

Day, Richard. "Sea-serpent, werewolf, etc." Vincennes (Ind.) *Valley Advance* (6 October 1981).

Day, Richard, and Paul Ingram. "Snakes beware! You don't want 'Big Jim's' fate." Vincennes (Ind.) *Valley Advance* (31 May 1983).

"The devil caught at last!" *Logansport* (Ind.) *Journal* (26 May 1849).

Eastern Puma Research Network, www.easternpumaresearch.com.

Eberhart, George. *Mysterious Creatures*. Santa Barbara: ABC-CLIO, 2002.

"Eurasian collared dove is the latest to invade state." Bloomington (Ind.) *Herald-Times* (11 November 2001).

Field Guide to the Birds of North America, 3d edition. Washington, D.C.: National Geographic, 1999.

"Fish from the clouds." *Newark* (Ohio) *Daily Advance* (4 August 1888).

"Fisherman catches one piranha, others spotted in Indiana lake." Bloomington (Ind.) *Herald-Times* (30 August 2000).

"5-foot lizard eludes capture in Brown County." *Indianapolis Star* (25 August 2001).

Fort, Charles. *The Complete Books of Charles Fort*. New York: Dover, 1974.

Freitag, Denise. "Cougar sighted in W. Harrison." *Dearborn County* (Ind.) *Register* (29 July 2005).

Freund, Paula. "Python's appearance in Yellowwood still unexplained." Bloomington (Ind.) *Herald-Times* (18 July 2001).

Gallegos, Alicia. "Blimey, mate. It was a kangaroo." *South Bend* (Ind.) *Tribune* (28 June 2005).

_____. "River gator shot by officials." *South Bend* (Ind.) *Tribune* (8 June 2005).

_____. "S.B. search called off for reported kangaroo." *South Bend* (Ind.) *Tribune* (14 July 2005).

Garner, Betty. *Monster! Monster!* Blaine, Wash.: Hancock House, 1995.

"Giant turtle?" *Indianapolis News* (15 July 1950).

Gillihan, Brad. "Emu 'lands' at area farm." *Bedford* (Ind.) *Times-Mail* (16 February 2002).

Glassing, Sandra. "Response to 'Officials seeking evidence of big cats prowling state.'" Bloomington (Ind.) *Herald-Times* (20 June 2006).

Green, John. *Sasquatch: The Apes Among Us*. Seattle: Hancock House, 1978.

Greenwell, J. Richard. "A classificatory system for cryptozoology." *Cryptozoology* 4 (1985): 1-14.

Gulf Coast Bigfoot Research Organization, www.gcbro.com.

Gutowski, John. "The Beast of 'Busco: An American Tradition." *Midwestern Folklore* 24 (Spring/Fall 1998): 1-147.

Halliday, Tim, and Kraig Adler, eds. *The Encyclopedia of Reptiles and Amphibians.* New York: Facts on File, 1991.

Harrison, Derek. "Ex-Marine relates 1982 creature encounter near Bedford." Knox County Folklore, Legends, and Tall Tales, rking.vinu.edu/folklore. htm.

Hartz, Brian. "Case of the Bigfoot sighting solved." Bloomington (Ind.) *Herald-Times* (19 December 2002).

_____. "Professor finds Bigfoot signs way off track." Bloomington (Ind.) *Herald-Times* (31 December 2002).

"'He looked like a big white tree limb.'" *Decatur* (Ind.) *Daily Democrat* (30 April 2004).

"Here, kitty, kitty." Bloomington (Ind.) *Herald-Times* (3 October 2004).

Hess, Bruce. "The Manitou Monster." *The Quarterly of the Fulton County Historical Society* 11 (February 1975):3-9.

Heuvelmans, Bernard. "What is cryptozoology?" *Cryptozoology* 1 (1982): 1-12.

Indiana Bigfoot Awareness Group, http://home.earthlink.net/ ~bigfoot46555.

"Indiana's big snake." *Fort Wayne* (Ind.) *Sentinel* (9 August 1895).

Johnson, Marda. "Fishermen snap up unexpected catch." *Mooresville-Decatur* (Ind.) *Times* (2 June 2006).

Jones, Pete. "Monster 'plagued' Miami County residents." *Peru* (Ind.) *Tribune* (8 September 2004).

"Judge rejects man's request to take turtles on tour." Bloomington (Ind.) *Herald-Times* (19 July 2002).

Keel, John. *The Complete Guide to Mysterious Beings.* New York: Doubleday, 1994.

Kirk, John. *In the Domain of the Lake Monsters.* Toronto: Key Porter, 1988.

Knox County Folklore, Legends, and Tall Tales, rking.vinu.edu/folklore. htm.

Koryta, Michael. "Exotic python pops up on Ellettsville porch." Bloomington (Ind.) *Herald-Times* (13 August 2002).

Kosky, Ken, and Elizabeth Holmes. "Cougar spotted west of city." Munster (Ind.) *Times* (24 December 2004).

Kunz, David. "Caiman seen in Patoka River." Jasper (Ind.) *Times-Mail* (2 August 2002).

LaGrange, Brad. "Black panther sighting." *North American BioFortean Review* 6 (May 2001): 27-28.

_____. "Black panthers in Perry County, Indiana." *North American BioFortean Review* 5 (December 2000): 4.

_____. "Cryptoherps of Indiana." *North American BioFortean Review* 1 (April 1999): 27.

_____. "Primates in Harrison County, Indiana?" *North American BioFortean Review* 1 (April 1999): 13.

"Latest snake story." *Marion* (Ohio) *Daily Star* (28 May 1891).

Leiser, Kan. "Mountain lion is taken off Missouri's endangered list." *St. Louis* (Mo.) *Post-Dispatch* (7 April 2006).

Leonard, Mike. "Woman finds iguana-retrieval services are in short supply." Bloomington (Ind.) *Herald-Times* (18 July 1995).

Lester, Todd. "Search for cougars in the East." *North American BioFortean Review* 7 (October 2001): 15-17.

Levco, Jessica. "WRT says, 'See ya later, alligator.'" Franklin (Ind.) *Daily Journal* (10 August 2005).

List of Fish Common Names, www.absoluteastronomy.com/enc2/list_of_fish_common_names.

"Lizard eludes would-be captors in Brown County." Bloomington (Ind.) *Herald-Times* (26 August 2001).

Lutz, John. "The black panther mystery." *North American BioFortean Review* 8 (March 2002): 35-40.

Mammal Species of the World, nmnhgoph.si.edu/msw.

"Man taking snapping turtle on tour." Bloomington (Ind.) *Herald-Times* (21 November 2002).

McLaren, George. "Hello, kitty? Hoosiers sight oversized cats." *Indianapolis Star* (20 February 2004).

"Meganthropus." Wikipedia, en.wikipedia.org/wiki/Meganthropus.

Miller, Jim. "Fancy footwork: Two Knox County men follow trail of big, mysterious creature." Vincennes (Ind.) *Sun-Commercial* (31 October 1982).

"The monster at Manitou." Cass County Historical Society and Museum, casscountyin.tripod.com/legends.htm.

"'Monster' or calf?" *Cincinnati Enquirer* (7 August 1960).

"Monsters of the deep." *Marion* (Ohio) *Daily Star* (26 August 1893).

"Mountain lion seized at home." Bloomington (Ind.) *Herald-Times* (24 September 1999).

"Mountain lion shot, killed after escaping from car after crash." Bloomington (Ind.) *Herald-Times* (2 February 2004).

"Mud mermaids." *Sandusky* (Ohio) *Register* (19 October 1894).

Newton, Michael. *Encyclopedia of Cryptozoology.* Jefferson, N.C.: McFarland & Co., 2005.

North American Mammals, www.mnh.si.edu/mna.

"Officials do not confirm reported cougar sighting." *Indianapolis Star* (5 May 2005).

Online Lake Cryptid Directory, dive.to/lakemonsters.

"Owen County couple say they saw panther." Bloomington (Ind.) *Herald-Times* (11 February 2006).

Perrin, D.L. "Big cats can cause ruckus." Goshen (Ind.) *Truth* (5 July 2005).

"Petersburg lays claim to 'gator killed downstate." *Indianapolis Star* (31 December 1946).

"Photo fuels false cougar rumors." Bloomington (Ind.) *Herald-Times* (18 April 2004).

Repine, Amanda. "The Beast of 'Busco." *Knot Magazine* (1 November 1999), www.knotmag.com/?article=16.

"Resembles a man." *Indianapolis Star* (1 May 1897).

Rife, Philip. *Bigfoot Across America.* Lincoln, Neb.: Writers Club Press, 2000.

"A sea serpent." *Vincennes* (Ind.) *Commercial Weekly* (22 April 1892).

"Sea serpent seen again." *Vincennes* (Ind.) *Commercial Weekly* (17 June 1892).

Seng, Phil, and Gwen White. Indiana Aquatic Nuisance Species Management Plan (1 October 2003), www.in.gov/dnr/invasivespecies/inansmanagementplan.html.

Shuker, Karl. "Alien zoo." *Fortean Times* 198 (August 2005): 18.

_____.*Mystery Cats of the World.* London: Robert Hale, 1989.

Simon, Thomas, John Whittaker Jr., John Castrale and Sherman Minton. "Revised checklist of the vertebrates of Indiana." *Proceedings of the Indiana Academy of Science* 111 (2002): 182-214.

Skinner, Charles. *Myths and Legends of Our Own Land.* Philadelphia: Lippincott, 1896.

Slabaugh, Seth. "Dead wolf found in local field." Muncie (Ind.) *Star Press* (5 August 2003).

Smalley, Donald. "The Logansport *Telegraph* and the monster of the Indiana lakes." *Indiana Magazine* 42 (1946): 249-267.

"Some say there is a cougar near town." Bloomington (Ind.) *Herald-Times* (14 May 2005).

Spangle, Beth. "Alligator confiscated from home." Bloomington (Ind.) *Herald Times* (9 September 1999).

"Strange animal 'ferocious as a tiger' baffles community." *Evansville* (Ind.) *Courier & Press* (29 November 1903).

Swaby, Bethany. "Strange fish caught at Griffy Lake." Bloomington (Ind.) *Herald-Times* (11 July 2001).

Swartz, Tim. "Mystery of the oil pit squids." *Strange Magazine* 18 (Summer 1997): 28-30.

"A tale of terror." *Fort Wayne* (Ind.) *Sentinel* (20 August 1879).

The Turtle in Missouri Folklore, websites.quincy.edu/~hoebiph/turtleman. html.

Van der Dussen, Kurt. "Animal mauls several dogs on northwest side." Bloomington (Ind.) *Herald-Times* (30 March 2006).

_____. "Anthropologist doubts creature is a sloth bear." Bloomington (Ind.) *Herald-Times* (6 February 2002).

_____. "Ape? Bear? Bigfoot? Sightings pose mystery." Bloomington (Ind.) *Herald-Times* (1 February 2002).

_____. "Big cat? Big dog? Animal sightings still a big mystery." Bloomington (Ind.) *Herald-Times* (17 May 2005).

_____. "Couple's dogs mauled." Bloomington (Ind.) *Herald-Times*(29 March 2006).

_____. "Crane officer reports he saw a big cat." Bloomington (Ind.) *Herald-Times* (24 May 2005).

_____. "Is a cougar on the prowl near Griffy?" Bloomington (Ind.) *Herald-Times* (11 May 2005).

_____. "Monitor lizard spotted near lake." Bloomington (Ind.) *Herald-Times* (25 August 2001).

_____. "Newspaper carrier reports black panther." Bloomington (Ind.) *Herald-Times* (28 June 2006).

_____. "Officials unaware of any cougar 'capture.'" Bloomington (Ind.) *Herald-Times* (25 May 2005).

_____. "Owen family: Panther killed pigs." Bloomington (Ind.) *Herald-Times* (9 February 2006).

_____. "Speculation continues on cougar near Griffy." Bloomington (Ind.) *Herald-Times* (12 May 2005).

_____. "Two more large cat sightings in Monroe." Bloomington (Ind.) *Herald-Times* (24 June 2006).

_____. "Wild cats...or wild imagination?" Bloomington (Ind.) *Herald-Times* (31 May 2006).

_____. "Woman sees cougarlike animal along Tapp Road." Bloomington (Ind.) *Herald-Times* (27 May 2005).

_____. "Woman spots 'huge cat.'" Bloomington (Ind.) *Herald-Times* (14 May 2005).

_____. "Woman trying to prove mystery critter's a cougar." Bloomington (Ind.) *Herald-Times* (18 May 2005).

Wilson, Doug. "Exotic cat spotted on Bloomington's east side." Bloomington (Ind.) *Herald-Times* (5 June 2002).

Wibert, Kathy. "'I got a good look'...Another Indiana Bigfoot tale." Vincennes (Ind.) *Sun-Commercial* (7 October 1979).

"A wild child." *Michigan City* (Ind.) *Gazette* (4 December 1839).

Willard, Shirley. "Tippecanoe River monster killed in 1872." *Fulton County Images* No. 5 (2000).

"Woman says what she saw looked like mountain lion." Bloomington (Ind.) *Herald-Times* (6 July 2002).

"Year of the cat." Bloomington (Ind.) *Herald-Times* (31 May 2006).